A Good Road to Walk

A Good Road to Walk

Reflections of a Presidential Scholar

Scott Neely

THE BENJAMIN WOFFORD PRIZE FOR NONFICTION

Holocene Publishing
Spartanburg, South Carolina

ISBN 1-891885-23-5
First printing, December 2000
Manufactured in the United States of America.

Design, typesetting, and publication consultant for Wofford College
by Olencki Graphics, Inc., Spartanburg, South Carolina.

Cover photograph—©2000 Scott Neely
Author photograph, back cover—©1999 Mark Olencki
Cover design—Mark Olencki

Holocene Publishing
John Lane, editor
Post Office Box 101, Wofford College
Spartanburg, South Carolina 29303

Table of Contents

Acknowledgments

If I have gleaned any lesson from my jaunt around the world, it is that no person journeys in isolation. Unable to list all of the teachers, waiters, and air traffic controllers who carried me safely back home, I am tempted to forgo any further effort at verbalizing my thanks. I am grateful.

Nevertheless, I would be remiss if I failed to mention a few individuals with whom I had close contact and who gave willingly of their time and of themselves for the benefit of my travels and my writing. I owe an incalculable debt to Dr. Joab Lesesne and Mrs. Janice Poole; to Dr. Bernie Dunlap, the Drs. Annemarie and Dennis Wiseman, and the Kopps; to Dr. Charles Kay and Dr. John C. Cobb for keen insight into thought, action, and craft; to David Streckfuss and Matt Cunningham; to Dr. Caroline Cunningham; to Dr. Larry McGehee and Mrs. Kathy Green; to Morningside Baptist Church and the First Presbyterian Church of Spartanburg, SC; to Rev. Talmage Skinner, Dr. Clarence Abercrombie, and the Tuesday afternoon vigils; to Chris Barrett and Karla Otroszko; and to my family.

I thank the donor for his generosity and his freedom of being.

And to Nancy Mandlove, David Schenck, Robert D'Erizans, Bindi Gandhi and Daryl Campbell, I give a warm and wordless smile.

To Joab Lesesne,
who housed it.

To Bernie Dunlap,
who praised it.

To Clarence L. Abercrombie,
who is it.

"If Ab can do it, you can do it too."
—Baker Maultsby and Peter Cooper

And the LORD said unto the Accuser, "Whence cometh thou?" Then the Accuser answered the LORD, "From going to and fro in the earth, and walking up and down it."

And the LORD said unto the Accuser, "Hast thou considered my servant...that there is none like him, a perfect and an upright man, that fearth God, and escheweth evil?"

Job 1:7-8

Introduction

There is a river, the streams whereof
Shall make glad the city of God...
God is in the midst of her;
She shall not be moved.
—Psalm 46:4-5

Founded in 1985 by an anonymous local philan-
thropist, the Wofford College Presidential International Scholarship annually asks one upperclass
student to design an independent project and to
carry it out in relevant countries around the globe.
The study usually revolves around institutions,
peoples, and issues of developing nations. The donor
has described the trip, which lasts approximately
eight or nine months, as a "combat experience,"
a way to throw the student into unfamiliar and trying
situations in order to learn, existentially, what the
world is like.

As vague and unsophisticated as such an approach
might seem, the mission of the scholarship constructed by the anonymous donor, in collaboration
with then President of Wofford, Dr. Joab Lesesne,
borders on the visionary. That the study is intended
to be more experiential than academic implicitly

encourages two modes of learning, interwoven and inseparable.

Upon receiving the scholarship, the donor tells the recipient to return with as few scars as possible. "Come back," he said to me over lunch one day, looking me straight in the eyes. In other words, I had received the opportunity to undertake this journey so that I could learn to respect the skills that living in the world necessitates.

I would learn that respect through life with others whose worlds differed greatly from my own and each other's. I would witness with my body how they lived, eating as they ate, sleeping where they slept. As my hosts, they would catch me when I fell. By managing to live through contact with and dependence on others so unlike me, I would see in turn what elements in their lives asked for the support that I could provide. In other words, at some point the traveler's education shifts from personal character building to involvement in the lives of others. The two types of learning, about self and about others, converge with the acceptance of responsibility—responsibility for life, not one's own and not that of theirs at one's expense, but for the life we share. At that point, the donor's challenge of making it in the world revolves around the world itself, and not the individual's trip.

"Look for saints!" my professor, Dr. Bernie Dunlap, exclaimed. With his hands behind his head, he rocked back in his chair. His body relaxed in thought but his eyes flitted nervously, chasing an idea. "How remarkable! What a great idea—to look at virtue by working with people who incarnate goodness. Really remarkable!"

I had come to his office to ask if he'd be willing to sponsor my trip. He readily accepted and leapt headfirst into a discussion I didn't feel ready to have.

"Have you thought about what you'd like to study?" he asked immediately. "It's such an amazing opportunity, and so well deserved."

"Thank you, thank you very much," I replied, feigning confidence. The recent public announcement of my reception of the scholarship had thrilled me, but I also felt intimidated. Called before the student body during opening convocation, my joy mingled with a sense of inadequacy. As I looked out into the crowd, I saw the faces of professors, far more deserving than I, who would never have this chance. My nomination meant that my classmates would never undertake this journey. I wondered what work they might have chosen had they received the scholarship and if I could conjure a project as brilliant as what they might have done. My joy and self-doubt combined to sweep clear from my mind every idea for a study I had thought of over the previous four years.

"Well, I've thought about it," I answered slowly. "Yes, but I don't really know yet what I'd like to do something with service maybe, or religion. I'm interested in the poor taking a leading role in problem solving, like self-empowerment, in a way."

Dr. Dunlap seized on my smudge of ideas and saw a defined form underneath. "It's really magnificent," he exuded. "You can study virtue! All those issues—empowerment, service, seeking the divine in our work."

"Go head hunting," I said, cutting in to try to follow him. I was seeing something now, as if a thousand disparate thoughts had suddenly aligned in a clear vision. It was so simple. "You mean that I could work with people who are virtuous."

"Who are virtue, even," he pushed the possibility further. "Exactly. And you can write about them."

I felt as if he had reached into my mind and dispersed a fog, opening a space for the light of ideas that could show me what to do. It was so obviously what I had wanted to undertake—to know the work of these people, to help them, to be close to them, perhaps to become like them. But I hadn't been able to conceptualize it.

From that point on, the details of the trip arranged themselves almost effortlessly. A volley of e-mails, letters and faxes produced a handful of invitations to places in which I could spend a month working with an individual or a group that exemplified goodness to those around them. A route around the world with eight month-long stops unfolded, and in early November of 1998, I left for Thailand.

There are many virtues that, like disciplines, move us toward one final good, the gift of ourselves to others. Beyond this, I can offer little else in the way of a verbalized philosophy defining the concept of virtue.

These stories, however, witness to that one goodness. It is my hope that where the heroes told of here fall short of perfection, their humanity will only render their inspiration stronger. All that they have done, all that they are, all that they hope to be is accessible to us.

By way of ending this introduction, I want to note that in the midst of all the striving for goodness that I have reported, happiness frequently filled the space around my hosts and me. Although I do not regard happiness as the ultimate point of our existence, it is an encouragement that comes to us as we try to better our lives. It seems most often to surround us when we find purpose, fulfillment, in what we are doing.

I hoped to write a happy book. I needed only to record the work of these people. Before going on this trip, I had not intended to publish, and I do not consider myself to be a writer. I believe there is other work asked of me. But in writing, I see that this project continues to seek to assist the good people with whom I spent my year of travel. And I felt especially privileged when I realized that to speak of the saints is to join in their work. My words, at least, I give to them, for goodness's sake.

Chiang Mai, Thailand

15 November 1998 – 18 December 1998

I came looking for you
At the edge of the city
In the house that you build
With bodies that will die,
With souls.

I saw a picture of the room in which Aeg lived before he came to die at the Friends for Life AIDS Hospice outside of Chiang Mai. When the phone call came from a child welfare worker informing the monks that some street kids were in need of help, they took a camera along to document the episode.

Phra Phongthep, the founder and director of the hospice, clicked to the next slide. We moved from the exterior of a dilapidated old building to its cavernous interior. Wires sprouting from the walls and exposing rebar hung flaccid over crumbling concrete. Moisture and mildew confused with shadows and crawled away from the camera's flash. Across the floor disheveled pallets lay in decently organized rows along the wall. A boy lay with his back to the lens.

He had on no pants, and a finger branched in from the left off camera to point to his thighs and bottom.

Lesions, red and purple, splotched his paling skin. For a moment I thought he'd been in a fight. The next slide zoomed closer to show welts wrapping from his groin and entering his rectum.

Aeg was either kicked out of his house or ran away from his family before he was nine years old. I failed to understand which was the case. Months later some friends of his walked up to a social worker concerned with street kids and child prostitution. They told her their friend was sick and needed help. She followed them to the building.

A whole colony of teenagers lived there, but spotting the one they were talking about was easy. He lay apart from everyone else. Lethargy, apathy, the inability to stand on his own strength, something kept him from even stirring when they walked up to him and she said hello. She went back to her car and called the monks at Friends for Life.

Phra Phongthep Dhammaguruko traveled a long road to his home at the hospice. Born to a poor family in Bangkok, he left after school for northeastern Thailand to work with farmers. Though he went to assist with progressive agricultural techniques through a non-governmental organization (NGO), he explained the move to me as a way to learn from the peasants' wisdom. He still holds to the Gandhian philosophy that human beings become divorced from themselves when separated from the earth. Stronger patients at his hospice water the plants twice a day. The gardens are the hospice. Banana trees grow next to the fences as well as in the farming plot proper; bougainvillea lopes around the roofs of the dormitory and the tuberculosis ward. While stretching our backs after transplanting a banana tree one day, he leaned on his shovel and smirked. "Making this hole takes us an hour." He pointed to what we had just filled in, then to the six other spots marked for digging. "An hour, a Buddhist monk and a student from USA. For Thai peasant-farmer—15 minutes. Thai technology!" he shouted, hoisting up the wooden handled hoe he held with his other hand. "No computer can beat it!"

I grinned and nursed my blossoming blisters.

Phra Phongthep's work with the farmers ended with a police investigation during the late 1970s. Accused of being a communist under the "suspicious evidence" that he had left the capital city for the country, he felt it best to leave his partners so as not to compromise the work with governmental interference. Frustrated with such headaches obstructing his efforts to help the poor, he entered the Thai Buddhist priesthood.

But he found the blessings of monasticism—the community life, the simplicity, the focus on freedom from prejudice and falsehood—sullied by abuse of the system. Laziness and excessive napping, unwillingness to work strenuously, and reliance on religious platitudes interfered with the help he thought his community could provide for themselves and for those around them. He enjoyed assisting families in need of counseling and comfort. But the other monks wearied him. Once while returning from the city we entered a tuk-tuk, a covered truck used to shuttle people throughout the district. We stepped in and I sat next to a dozing monk. He wore pink and orange robes, freshly cleaned and unfaded, with a saffron sack tucked under his arm. Sweat trickled across his nose. He snored loudly once, then sighed into deeper sleep. Phra Phongthep looked at me, smirking. My laughter at this woke the monk, who grinned sheepishly and tried to stay awake the rest of the short trip.

Nevertheless, Phra Phongthep had remained a monk for twelve years. He would wake late at night to practice vipassanna meditation on his bedroll, his fellow monks dreaming around him. When his attentiveness fatigued he would stroll the temple grounds, practicing walking meditation or enjoying the moon, the night dog calls, the cestrum nocturnum.

But with the development of AIDS in Thailand, he felt the need to leave. When his abbot refused to provide care for the sick and his brothers declined to follow him in the new work, he broke with the monastic system. Another monk had returned to the order after contracting HIV, and together they joined to form the Friends for Life Hospice outside of Chiang Mai.

Phra Phongthep and Phra Au lifted Aeg into their truck and returned to the hospice. He did not stay long, dying a few months after his arrival. I saw a few slides from that period. He did not smile in any of them. He did face the camera.

I came to the hospice as a volunteer and so I cannot presume to know what it was like for Aeg to enter the community. But I imagine it as similar to the end of my first full day.

The night before I'd made my bed and lain down in the nine o'clock dark, listening to pneumonic coughing in surrounding rooms. The next day I stumbled around trying to understand what plants were to be soaked and which sprinkled in the morning and evening watering periods. With few jobs needing immediate care I passed the day reading people, watching them come in and out of the gate, dutifully fulfilling a handful of chores and then languishing about with nothing to do. Four times I walked behind the partition in the back of my room to the concrete floor and toilet, trying to figure out how and where to bathe. At five a man stepped to the screen door and called me. "Mister, mister, prayer now!" I emerged from the bathroom and he smiled, taking my hand and leading me around a cluster of trees drowning in mandevilla. People were gathering in the small temple beside the lower pond, pulling mats from a pile and seating themselves on the floor. One of the patients smiled as I walked in and called for a couple of mats to be given to me. My guide pointed to the upper right corner of the linoleum floor, then laid the mats out for me, positioning the four corners with squares in the tiling. I nodded thanks and sat heavily. Laughter came from the back and I blushed at my awkwardness. Somebody hissed a reprimand, then giggled too.

The little meditation hall was perhaps the most beautiful building I had ever seen. Once seated, I saw the tiling to be a plastic sheet with square print rolled out the length of the floor and curving up to cover the raised stoop in front. The left half of this stoop hosted an altar. A fat little Buddha chuckled at the knees of a graceful if squat larger one, more serene and concentrated. Flowers, purple and cone-shaped white, wilted and bent down. Votive candles of uncoordinated height spread across the stoop's lip.

Phra Au and Phra Phongthep had built the temple from spare slats of lumber and screening. Little more was needed—they'd poured a concrete floor and posted the wood along the perimeter, nailing a screen wall around it. Corrugated steel funneled rain and nuts off the roof. Inside the monks had tacked their old saffron robes from the roof's pitched center to the top wall beams, the Holy of Holies parted like yellow water. Rats had chewed through in places, and mosquitoes filtered in, moaning around us.

Phra Au came in and seated himself on the stoop next to the Buddha statuette. He gazed at me, smiled encouragingly, then gained an austere solidity and stared over the gathering heads. Booklets were being passed around, and my neighbor opened the beautiful and incomprehensible Thai text for me to follow. Thai characters are very blocky but curl into flourishes as they finish. They reminded me of my father's stacked spice box after he lets the basil go to seed. In three and a half weeks, after a transliteration had been completed with the help of another patient named Aeg, I would be able to almost complete the entire vespers service. That first night left me blushing in foolishness but ecstatically happy with where I found myself. The room settled and chanting began. I started to feel my ankles boring into the floor.

> *Yo so pahkahwah arahang samah samputo*
> *Sahwahkahto yainah pahkahwahtah tahmo*
> *Supatepahno yahsah pakahwah to sahwahkahsangho*

What this meant and how long it would continue

eluded me. I couldn't determine the beginning and ending of the service, much less what page we were on. But it mattered little. The words meshed and droned in my head, drowning out the mosquitoes and dizzying me. Then a tightening muscle along my spine twitched and shuddered me awake. In the distraction I looked out the screen to see Phra Phongthep scooting by on his bicycle. He would ride it from one building to another, maybe twenty yards in full distance, dinging a little bell and cackling at his foolishness. He claimed it helped him get to work faster. He sped under a covered walk and I turned back to the chanting, shifting one leg behind me and rubbing my ankles. The man beside me peeked at my movement and quickly patted my knee, teasing me for my softness.

Ahnuh tah lo potet sah tahm mah sahlahte
Sahtah tai wah muhnuh sah nahng puhttoh pahkahwah —
D'thay.

Occasionally the unison of chanting dropped with an outbreak of coughing. It would wrack the person's body and cause him to bend over, almost lying down in his own folded lap. Then a tissue would come out, the excess would be wiped away, and the hum picked up again in whatever corner of the room it had been lost.

The chant ended and Phra Au closed his eyes. After a moment he opened them quickly to motion to me that this would be a quiet time, that my hands should be folded in this manner. His eyes shut again and he receded, motionless. Scattered coughing passed around the room and others rustled about trying to regain some semblance of comfort. The mosquitoes resumed where our voices had left off. I listened in the quiet. Our breathing formed a full unity that my absence in chanting had prevented. The smiles of encouragement, the guidance to my place, had brought me to sit and breathe with these strangers for a few weeks. We resumed a short chant and the sit ended.

As I collected my mats and folded them to store, my guide strutted over. "Important to bathe," he said straightforwardly, then pulled at my unwashed hair. "Get a bucket, then water," and he motioned scooping and dumping water over himself as he stuttered the instructions. I laughed with understanding at the little dance he had gotten himself into and mimicked it. "Yes, yes, with water!" he exclaimed, then rubbed his arms as if he were shivering. "But not now!" he teased back, mocking my dirtiness in the night's chill. Nevertheless, he walked back to my room and showed me the drain in the concrete floor. We exited and he scrambled around in a shed for two buckets. Slipping the rusted cover off a blue oil drum brimming full of clean water, he started filling my buckets. "This, this, this," he said, explaining the motion.

"Yes," I nodded at the obviousness of the solution, and when he saw I'd gotten the idea, he flicked me with a handful of water and scampered off into the dark. I finished filling the buckets and went back to my room.

Darkness covered us and I slipped off my clothes. Already I struggled to place as little of my foot on the chilly floor as possible, relishing the thought of water

down my back. For a moment I held my breath—
I could hear television channels being switched,
announcers giving way to an opera singer; a telephone rang and Phra Phongthep answered, paused,
responded; dogs wandered off somewhere to howl;
the wind lifted and a radio came on. In the hospice
there was night, there were crickets. I lifted the first
bucket. Water shot down.

"Sc-hat!" Phra Phongthep called from my screen
door.

"Yes?" I shivered out, reaching hopelessly for my
towel hanging in the undifferentiated darkness.

"Movie tonight! Come to the porch! Tonight—
Eddie Murphy!"

Scrubbing down, rinsing up, toweling off as
quickly as I could, I pulled on my clothes and went
out to join the others.

The slides of Aeg that I saw showed a thirty year
old's eyes looking out of a gaunt, six year old body.
His cheeks pulled back like a taut kite above his
stringy neck. During Phra Phongthep's presentation
about AIDS in Thailand and the necessity of caring
for the suffering, Aeg became a mythic personality.
He stared through the projector bulb like a boy blind
and captured, first by alienation from his family, then
by the sickness, then by the camera. Every click of the
remote control threw him up on the wall in a beatific
light, as if his suffering could give me something. He
made a lonely picture.

But in every shot of him at the hospice someone
accompanied him, older patients who played with
him or cared for him or simply lounged under the
trees. He never lost his loneliness, but a certain

company joined him.

In that slide presentation Phra Phongthep addressed the group of foreign exchange students with whom I'd arrived at Friends for Life. They had come to learn about causes of and responses to AIDS in northern Thailand, the nation's region considered most affected by the spread of HIV. I'd come to stay with my first saint, to hear what he had to say about meeting problems and being virtuous, and to see how he matched up with those words. Earlier, while speaking with my Thailand contact, a foreign study director named David Streckfuss, I'd described the trip as a trick. "It's true that I'll be an interruption in the lives of these people. And it must be somewhat difficult to have a foreign kid trailing you around, testing your efficacy and integrity in meeting problems, waiting to see how you respond. But somebody'll meet the test, and that'll be worth witnessing."

"Are you sure you aren't setting up a straw man?" he asked. "Doesn't every action have a certain amount of virtue in it, a little goodness even if it's hard to see? Do you think your presumptions make your study fair? Maybe you should pick seven or eight people at random to match your eight chosen saints, compare what kind of people they are and what they do, how virtuous they are."

The questions irritated me a bit and I didn't follow all of his thinking because of my frustration. I hadn't met anyone who'd second-guessed my premises, and here my contact had nudged me a little to see if I really knew where I was going. Of course I didn't.

"Maybe, maybe—after all, our e-mails and this

conversation could serve as an example. I could write about you as one of the random eight."

He grinned and bobbed his head away, then turned back. "Anyway, you're right about being something of an interruption." He paused long enough to disconcert me. "The monk you want to work with usually asks our group after his presentation if anybody is up to the job of staying and working in the hospice. He likes to poke at us, and I thought we'd wait till then to ask if you can join him for a few weeks." I looked worriedly out the window and wondered how long I'd be in Thailand.

A week later while waiting for the presentation to begin, I'd watched the monk flurry about the meeting room, trying to size him up and determine whether or not he would have me. "You have come too early!" he jeered at the group. "So you must wait two minutes for the tape to rewind." He ducked back under the table to finish plugging in the cassette player.

The problems of prostitution, of husbands transmitting HIV to wives and through impregnation to children, of "recruiters" pulling boys and girls into prostitution rings on the pretense of employing them to relieve their families' debts, had been explained to us by a social worker we'd previously visited. Phra Phongthep turned to the difficulties facing Thai families in caring for their friends and relatives.

"Those who would call themselves 'human' must love others. There is a difference between being a human and being a person, a biological person."

I thought this a good beginning for a moralist if not for a saint. Learning to be a human at the beginning of the trip was something to which I could look forward.

"Here there are three jobs. Number one, we must sew cadavers of patients who have just died, then give them shots and carry them to the crematorium." He clicked to the first slide. A pair of hands supported a prostrate patient's back as another pair gloved in latex laced skin with thread and needle. The image wasn't frightening and without his commentary we would not have recognized what we were seeing. But we understood, and the room silenced a bit more. Another slide of a truck implied the route to the crematorium.

"Number two, we must help people with problems of defecation and clean them up, in their beds, in the toilets, and cleaning their diapers." In the pictures a shirtless man smiled up at the camera while another crouched over a tub. In the series of slides that followed he never looked up, though the assistant waved a diapered hello at the photographer.

Phra Phongthep clicked to a scene of a blue mountain over banana trees. "Number three, we must dig big holes," and he threw his arms out to form a canyon's mouth, "and plant the trees, the banana trees." He mimed plopping a baobab into the ravine and wiped his hands. Bougainvillea splintered the next frame.

"We try to get other groups that help people with AIDS to establish hospices like this one. It is not hard to do if you have some funding, because here the stronger residents take care of the weaker ones. But no one has done this after us. There is never any response."

He explained that there were only ten people in

the hospice at a time, perhaps eleven. One slept outside the hospice. Many groups wanted Friends for Life to expand, but he feared that would promote the abandonment of people with AIDS, which was exactly contrary to the fundamental idea. He wasn't a sponge for problems others didn't want to confront. The slides changed from buildings at the hospice with camera-drunk patients in the foreground to a woman in bed. "The goal is families and communities caring for their sick. The center serves just as a small example." In a succession of pictures, the woman was transferred from her bed to a metal stretcher, then brought to the side of a red truck. A monk and another man lifted her into the cab, then returned the stretcher to the truck bed.

"It would be better," he said, "if there were a few centers around, some in each province, to teach how to care for the sick and provide care for the very poor and those without families." But there was only this one in the North. He flipped through a few slides of the hospice. In one the corner of a smiling face blocked the right side of the photo. Behind, a row of hospital beds showed a handful of people lying down, oblivious to the photographer's intentions. One head poked furtively above the railing of a bed.

Another slide spread across the wall, again of a woman in a bed. "The most common problem," Phra Phongthep continued, his voice a little more focused, harsher, "is that a related person is not willing to accept the responsibility of caring for someone, so they must come here. Sometimes it is a family, a mother or a husband, sometimes it is a doctor at the hospital."

"This woman, her family helped her to bed one night. Then three days later a neighbor came into the home and found everything gone. No one was there except this woman. Her family put her to bed and cleared out the entire house, all of the furniture and everything. They left because they didn't want to help her. So she came here, and we tried to find her family. We wanted to tell them that we could not care for everyone, that they had to care for this woman from their family. That is why we have so few beds at Friends for Life. But we could not find them."

"Fear is the most common reason for this. We have no cure here. Nobody survives—the only question is how quickly we die. The important thing is how quickly we die. As far as pain goes, there are times when we can't do anything—even doctors can't always do something."

"In November 1993 we started this hospice to care for people rejected and discriminated against by society. In that first year I assumed that the cause that made people discriminate was fear of contraction. But then with time, more and more hospitals sent their patients here. They said the families wouldn't take the people back and they wouldn't keep them either. Then I understood another fear for doctors and administrators and families—fear of care and increased costs."

"Then even AIDS support groups started to send people here. They would talk about the disease but not care for people, and even some of their workers were sent here by their friends. I think now it is a reflection of our fear of dirtiness rather than of contraction. People just don't want to deal with disease.

We see this also with lepers and cancer patients. Sometimes now we even refuse people if their families can care for them. But we will give them advice on how to help and what doctors to see."

"Our human society has still not enough compassion. One day we too will become sick and we will need help and assistance from others."

For a moment, everyone in the room breathed. A hand went up.

"Yes?"

"How do you keep your spirits up through all of this?"

His seriousness fell away but his moral gravity remained under a growing smile. "If I wasn't doing this I don't know what I would do. Be a layperson, have a job... I have already done that! There, there is no happiness. One condition of being a monk, we have free food, clothing, and medical treatment in the hospital." His smile slackened a bit and his voice softened. "And I am able to do more now to help other people. The Lord Buddha taught that the life of helping others is the life of happiness. That is why I am here today. There is no better way to live than this."

The projector light went off and the fan whirred. We collected our notebooks, filed past a porch and went downstairs to a covered area. In back two tables met, covered with pots of rice and hot vegetables. Around the floor's edge in a wide, incomplete circle a scraggly group of men sat cross-legged. We were to share dinner with the residents of Friends for Life.

Uneasiness divided the group as we served ourselves and ate. At the slide show's end, our deepest sense of virtue and a hunger for justice had been stirred. We were all ready to shave our heads and eyebrows to become monks, catch the first flight home, and found hospices devotedly modeled after Phra Phongthep's. But the slide show's subjects disoriented us. Our best desires had been evoked and there we sat, speechlessly gaping at the very people for whom we felt legitimate empathy despite our differences. And they stared back at us, confused by our presence, wondering what we thought, maybe intimidated by our health or wealth, maybe just apathetic.

Phra Phongthep bent over to the man sitting next to him and whispered something in his ear. The man leaned closer and almost fell in the monk's lap. Phra Phongthep caught him, righted him, and yelled back, "Hey, did you know there are foreigners eating with us tonight?!"

Everyone looked at the snickering monk. The man scooted closer and said, "What?"

"There are foreigners eating with us tonight!" he yelled and then, for our benefit, motioned to his ears. "He cannot hear much!" he chortled. The other residents were giggling and pointing at the show. We students looked around to see how we should react.

"No, I didn't know," the man replied. "Where?" He craned his neck around, trying to see us with little success despite the two pair of bottle-bottom thick glasses propped on his nose. Phra Phongthep made circles with his fingers and placed them over his own eyes, acting blind.

"They are all around us! And did you know," he lowered his voice to a faux-confidential level, "that three beautiful women are sitting next to you?"

"Oh no, oh no, get them away from me," the man cried, spilling his soup as he stood hurriedly. "Get them away from me!" Once on his feet he started stumbling about the patio, walking straight towards a group of women across the floor from him. He ran into a wall and turned, only to run into another. Phra Phongthep followed him. He grabbed him by the shoulders, spun him, misdirected him, tickled him. The game began to look like a sadistic bastard-ization of pin-the-tail on the donkey.

"Why run away? They are right here!" The entire room had given up on concern with the impropriety of the fiasco and roared in laughter. I sat, sides aching from the situation's hilarity, wondering what sin I had committed to be thrown in with such a saint as this.

"Get me away from them, get me away! It's stand-ing too close to women that got me in this mess!" The room burst into laughter at the shameless truth of his remark, but the monk resumed a pastoral mode. He put his arm around the man and straight-ened him into place. The man grinned at the faint laughing that reached him and strained to see who sat nearby. Phra Phongthep tickled him a little, unwilling to let the joke go, and then smiled next to his ear.

"Do you really believe that?" he asked.

Although his remark may have failed to remember the important theological concept of confession, and although the group as a whole took little notice of his statement, I felt that the consolation offered by Phra Phongthep to the patient involved something more than easy absolution. His words pushed the moment towards real grace. Phra Phongthep knew the man. He knew why he was there and that the man thought of his sickness everyday. He had suffered from his own reprimanding enough. The important understanding between the men was that they were together and that this was good. For a while they could enjoy each other, care for each other, even love each other until the day when they would go apart. The joking evinced companionship.

The laughter settled to conversation, extending even to broken words between residents and visitors. Phra Phongthep put his hand on the man's shoulder and they took their seats again. He said nothing more, leaving off with his nudge to go further than self-pity and blame, to look a little more deeply.

But Phra Phongthep couldn't hold his peace for long. "Where's the monk?" he asked, squatting right beside the man.

"Over there," responded the blind man, pointing past the monk toward the tables.

"How do you know he's over there?"

"I can hear him over there," answered the deaf man. Our laughter again filled the patio.

"Yes, but now I'm right here," said the monk, relinquishing the joke out of pity for the patient. He placed his hand on the old man's shoulder again. He looked at us, then back to the man. Everyone continued laughing, caught between ridicule and horror at the monk's delight in his own show of insensitivity.

"Good, good," said the man. "Stay close so that I won't be alone anymore—"

Our laughter broke a second and we saw a little more, a little more clearly.

The sexual energy filling a place so poorly treated by sexuality always surprised me. A young Japanese student with only a smidgen more Thai than I came by one afternoon for supper in order to see the community. It was something to see the cheer that her showing up—light-skinned, young, exotic, struggling in Thai and generally very beautiful—created. Compared to her newness I was made to feel like a veteran in the hospice, and having a compatriot in foreignness was nice. While washing dishes I heard numbers being grasped at, a mouth trying to get words around an idea, and a burst of laughter just after my name and age. The words "Sc-hat, yee-sip-song," were distinctly said—"Scott, twenty-two". Everybody around the table popped around the wall corner to twinkle their eyes at me, and the Japanese woman just stood there, thin and bashful and thoroughly bewildered. Apparently we made quite a pair, neither speaking the other's language.

Delighted with the matchmaking game, Phra Phongthep came into the vespers hall just before meditation. He had decided it was my turn for chastisement. I squatted awkwardly on a stack of mats offered by a compassionate resident who must have seen me sweating blood in previous services. He knelt beside me, taking gentle but firm hold of my arm.

"S-chat," he grinned, looking around to see who was paying audience, "what do you think of Taiko? You laugh when you met her—what you think?"

I turned my elbow and took his arm in my hand,

matching his grasp with my own. His eyes lit with delight at my audacity. "Taiko...I thought...I thought she was nice." I paused thoughtfully. "And you, what did you think of Taiko?"

Now he was at the heart of his joy, challenged with the same kind of discomforting humor he loved. A random U.S. American student was testing him, a revered man of the cloth. His little boy eyes gleamed at the proximity of danger. He could feel everyone waiting. Even those with no English could understand this exchange solely from the word 'Taiko'.

"I think, I say 'No Comment'!" he laughed. He jumped up and slapped me jokingly on the shoulder.

"Uh, like a president—," I nudged sarcastically.

"Like President Clinton!" He neared ecstasy then, joyous at the comparison between an obscure Buddhist monk dedicated to work with AIDS who had caught a glimpse of a moderately attractive Japanese woman, and the infamous philandering President of the United States. "Like President Clinton! No comment! No comment!"

A recurrent problem plagues non-government organizations. Though often flooded with eager volunteers, few of the good souls willing to serve have sufficient skill to really help. Their virtue flounders and impedes due to an absence of proper training. My situation at Friends for Life matched the pattern exactly. Excited to work with Buddhist monks and AIDS patients, I nonetheless lacked any knowledge of the problems facing residents and of the solutions practiced by the monks. My medical training amounted to first aid learned as a Boy Scout.

I would approach Phra Phongthep every morning to ask what I could do that day. I was ready, my spirit generous, but he could not take time from his frenzied schedule to teach me how to do what needed doing. In three weeks I would leave. I was welcome. I was accepted. But I was temporary.

After finishing my daily assigned task of sweeping the dirt road looping the hospice grounds, I'd seek him out to see if there was anything further that I could do.

"What can you do?" he would ask, seriously searching and eventually seriously exasperated.

"Not much," I'd shrug, half honing false humility and half joking at my shortcomings.

I began poking around the hospice looking for some job that would be of help, something more than a simple occupation of time. I chopped peppers in the kitchen, then scrubbed the dishes. I chased chickens from the yard. I moved tables to the offices. I moved them back to the infirmary. I wondered if I was anything other than a burden. But the monk smiled delightedly when one morning
I asked for a stepladder to mend the fabric ceiling in the meditation hall.

"Many people will thank you," he beamed approvingly, putting his hands on his hips and craning his neck to inspect the rat holes. "No more mosquitoes! Many people will be grateful, yes." He looked back at me through professorial spectacles, slapped me on the shoulder, and walked out of the screened temple.

All morning I worked, and for the first time I felt completely satisfied at Friends for Life. I'd found a task in need of doing and undertaken it. Its usefulness pleased me. Without the mosquitoes we would more easily maintain our concentration during meditation. The patients could focus on their breath without flinching from a bite every few seconds. Clergy and laity at the hospice would all attain everlasting peace and enlightenment thanks to my neat sewing job. It was all worth the fear I felt, beating the rats in the curtains back with a broom after every few stitches. The sun slanted through holes in the roof and marked the floor with spots of quiet orange light.

Late in the morning Phra Phongthep came back into the temple and called to me. As I descended the ladder he came into the temple, letting the screen door slam and rattle.

"Now, Sc-hat," he said. The mischief in his eyes had subsided and he showed a kind of fatherly purpose in his words.

"Yes," I said, bowing my head slightly.

"I have a job for you. Tomorrow you will go with Au to the infirmary. You know Jarune?" I had watched Jarune, one of the weaker patients, stiffly making his way from bed to table, then back to bed twice a day, in the morning and at noon. He walked a slow, measured gait, taking time to step over dirt clods and pebbles in his path as if they barred his way. He combed his wavy hair to the side and its thickness seemed disproportionately large in comparison with his shallow cheeks. "You will help him because he needs his wounds cleaned." Phra Phongthep gestured to his inner thighs, his left calf, his shoulder. "Because of infection. No infection, so we must clean. And Au will teach you. Tomorrow. Ten o'clock. Okay?"

"Everyday?" I asked.

"Everyday," he said with satisfaction, and he grinned at the eagerness in my voice.

The next morning Phra Au stuck his head into the temple where I was still working and called me to follow him. In the infirmary he handed me a surgical mask and a pair of latex gloves.

"For you. Every...every day." He pushed through his elementary English, far more sophisticated than the meager Thai I'd managed to acquire, to teach me. I understood the importance of his words. I needed to use these. Jarune's wounds needed to stay clean and so did I.

Moving from cabinet to cabinet he attentively turned locks and selected the glass bottles he required. With cotton balls soaked blue with alcohol he swabbed the inside of a couple of shallow metal dishes, then their outside, then a pair of large tweezers. In one bowl he poured a mixture of hydrogen peroxide and saline solution, showing me the correct amounts. The other brimmed with alcohol.

He carefully placed everything on a shiny steel tray and carried it outside. With his chin he motioned for me to pull a second table up to a pair of white benches and set the tray on it, signaling what to place where, in what order each instrument should be set out. A little radio played variations of static on a table behind us.

Just as he finished arranging everything, the door to the tuberculosis ward scraped open and Jarune hobbled out toward us. His feet in flip-flops shuffled with each step. He hardly bent his knees and never stepped very far in front of himself. He looked down to assure himself of his next steps, then stared straight ahead, vaguely, and moved forward.

He wore a faded green windbreaker, similar to an old Members Only jacket, against the mild Thai November. A frayed white towel wrapped around his lower body. Over his right eye a large patch of cotton gauze puffed out, the edges taped tight across his cheek, nose bridge, and over his eyebrow.

He lay down on the two white benches pulled more or less parallel and flush, easing back to find a balance as they wobbled under his weight. For a moment he adjusted his head, scrunched his shoulders and relaxed them into place, and closed his eyes. One hand rested on the bench, but with the other he reached down slowly to his waist and untied the towel's knot. He removed one flap, folded back the other and lay shivering slightly, naked, waiting.

Phra Au and I watched the process without speaking or moving as if assisting at a rite to which we had not expected admission. Phra Au's face set with grimness and compassion.

In Thailand, a nickname often substitutes for a person's given name in everyday use. "Au" denotes the gentleness with which a mother breastfeeds her infant. The name described the man's actions perfectly.

Born to a poor family and taught to carve wooden statuettes for tourists, Au's aversion to Buddhism changed after a series of conversations with a priest and he became a monk in his late teenage years. When he heard about Phra Phongthep's work, Au left his monastery for a far more austere and engaged life at the hospice. Every movement he makes communicates happiness, as if the satisfaction of his work so saturates his muscles that he remains constantly at rest.

We enjoyed each other, each admiring the other's journey and the possibilities held therein. Sometimes he would join me on a high porch at night. I would read there until late and he would sit with me, not speaking, just pleased that we were together. He was twenty-five and I twenty-two, and a friendship formed easily between us.

After gazing at Jarune a moment longer, Au began to move. White gauze covered patches of Jarune's legs from his groin down to his Achilles tendons. In other places lesions showed bare, purple and red. His skin was dry, and its cracking pulled so tightly that some of the sores had opened, flowers maturing from buds. A few bled lightly. Phra Au began gingerly removing the bandages and more wounds showed. They glistened with a thin covering of clean secretion. As he removed the dressings some tore.

Slowly, Au began to work. He swabbed each open lesion carefully with the hydrogen peroxide-saline solution, dabbing a fresh cotton ball into the bowl and lightly cleansing the open flesh and skin around it. As each was cleaned he covered the wound with a new gauze patch and taped it down. Those that had remained closed for a few days he did not treat, hoping that they would continue to heal.

Then came the eye. The bandage was pulled back to show a top lid so swollen that only the thinnest rim of white eyeball showed under his lashes. The darting pupil flinched sensitively to the light.

Phra Au cleaned the surface and edges of the lids with a Q-tip dipped in the saline and peroxide. Mucus collected on the cotton end and pulled to the corner of the eye. A yellow crust stuck to the tip as well. Cleaning required several rounds with the Q-tip and Jarune's eyes squinched ceaselessly, trying without success to escape the pressure of Phra Au's attention.

Work on the eye required more time than all that had been devoted to his lower body. As he worked, Phra Au openly chastised Jarune for rubbing his eye or failing to sponge both his legs well. Occasionally he would turn to me to make certain that I followed his actions and understood what to do. I nodded a constant assent to every motion. When Au had finished taping the last end of the eye bandage he turned to me with questioning eyes to see if anything further needed explanation. Behind him, Jarune slid awkwardly off the bench and made his way back to bed inside the white building.

"It's good, it's good," I said to Au. "Thank you. Thank you. I see." I pointed to my head, my eyes, to where Jarune had lain, I motioned with my hand to show that I had learned how to clean lesions, I smiled.

"Oh, oh," he said. "Good."

After a few more mornings, I did understand what I needed to do. I undertook the work with great purpose, understanding it as the primary reason for my stay at the hospice. I thought, sometimes, that it had been ordained that I should come to work at Friends for Life just so I might serve Jarune. As I moved over his body I tried to see him as Christ, suffering and blessing me; then as the Buddha, giving himself to call me into wakefulness; then as a member of the interdependent system of life to whom I had become especially connected. To a degree, my imagination of him in such religious terms helped me to see him as more than just a body bleeding slowly on two white benches.

But in the end Jarune was a man, and I was able to help him somewhat. Constant contact with someone brings us into a special relationship with him or her in the way that a couple may grow inseparably close through marriage. The space Jarune and I shared was intimate. With no verbal means of communication, we moved quickly to other ways of understanding. As I cleaned his sores I watched his muscles for twitches and flinching, whatever would indicate that I pressed too hard, that I hurt him, that he felt comforted. If his eyes curled back into his head, I had caused pain to the person I wanted to help. Phra Au had taught me how to use the tools correctly. Jarune taught me how to do the job.

Every morning at ten I would come out of the infirmary with the silver tray, and my clattering signaled him to join me on the porch. He lay; I worked; we spent an hour together. At every morning's end I would bend toward him and say, more like a breath than a word, muffled almost inaudibly through my mask, "Okay."

"Krup-kuhn-krup," he would answer, thanking me and bowing though prostrate, and then he would return to the tuberculosis ward.

One day a few weeks later, another man, Prichya, walked out of the low building and sat on a tattered stool, apart from us and watching. I hardly noticed him and only motioned a cheery hello minutes after his arrival. He waved back.

I could not know then that he would ask me for help when my work with Jarune finished. Embarrassed to show anyone, a large lesion on his penis had opened and become so infected that pus, yellow with a slight greenish coloring, showed under part of the raw skin. No one had attended to it because no one but he knew it was there. When I cleaned it he spoke to me in broken English to maintain composure. As I touched the peroxide-soaked cotton to his skin he seethed in pain, writhing almost erotically, and scrambled to find a distraction, to say something to show that he was undeterred. He spurted nonsensical strings of elementary school English vocabulary.

I could not know that in another week, only a few days before my departure, I would wake to find him missing. When I asked about him, Phra Phong-thep did not smile.

"Sent to the hospital," he said in a matter-of-fact tone that did not lack in harshness. "For pneumonia." He turned away.

In that time I worked, vaguely aware of Prichya watching, concentrated on Jarune. Morning rain beat on the porch roofing.

"Scott," Prichya called.

I looked up and smiled at him. "Yes, Prichya."

"Hand," he said and stretched his hand forward, moving it in a circle over the ground.

"Yes, Prichya, this is a hand. This is my hand." I flexed my fingers, thinking he wanted to practice and perhaps show off some of his English. But he looked at me with serious eyes.

"No," he said. "Hand."

"Yes," I said.

"No," he restated. I could feel his earnestness across the few yards separating us. He leaned forward on the stool seat and said, "The hand of God."

In that moment I could not work any more, and I could do nothing but work. The reality of what he had seen and of what he would ask of me in only a few minutes tore my previous conception of my trip in two, like a temple curtain ripped suddenly down the middle.

Discovering, in my own body, the possibility of what we might be to another became my vocation.

But the most beautiful moment in Chiang Mai came days later. As I turned to come up from the upper pond, two buckets sloshing over with oily water tearing my arms out of socket, I saw Jarune. He sat slouched in a wheelchair with his head bent far back. Water poured through his hair and shampoo foamed around the tires and his ankles.

Behind him stood a woman, her face expressionless but intent, moving her fingers along his scalp.

I had wondered about Jarune's past, about what he had done before his illness, how he had contracted HIV, how long he had been infected before becoming so manifestly sick. Even with concerns for politeness aside, no means existed for me to learn his story from him. I let the questions subside.

When I saw the couple, I knew she was his wife. Her hands in his hair understood too much for the situation to be otherwise.

I could not tell if she was sick, if he had infected her or she him, or if he was at the hospice simply because she could not afford the care he needed.

I did not know if she was angry or to what degree she grieved.

It did not matter. Something had brought them as close as any two human beings might hope to be.

The Saints

A guest arrived for a few nights' stay at the hospice, and my room was made available to her. I would sleep on the second-story porch where I read at night and into which trees climbed.

"Scott!" Phra Au called to me from the bottom stair. When my head appeared over the railing he vigorously rubbed his hands over his torso and under his arms as if soaping himself. He nodded questioningly, and I shook my head in affirmation. Without my own bedroom, I was to bathe with the monks.

Under the stairs stood two plastic barrels, at least three feet high each, full of rainwater. A yellow bowl like a dog food dish sailed lazily across the water's surface in one of them.

Already in the night I shivered. I stripped down to my shorts as Phra Au folded his robe around his waist, making it into a sarong.

"Okay?" he asked, almost childishly. The water laughed at us in the night chill, and that we were about to take its dare thrilled him.

I looked at him—gentle, taut muscled and beautiful, head hair and eyebrows freshly shaven, and chattered out, "Ok-kay…"

He yelped like a nipped dog as the first bowlful shot down his spine.

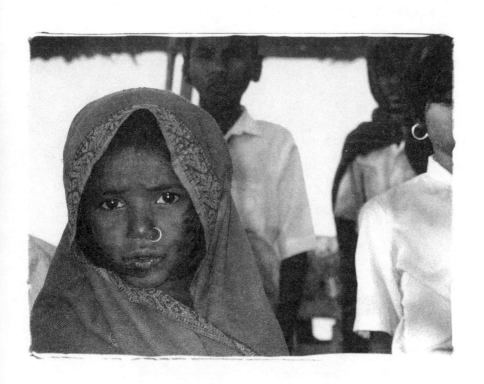

Bodh Gaya, Bihar, India

14 December 1998 – 20 January 1999

The muddy bones of poverty,
the broken people—

all this we built
and will raze.

I left Friends for Life in the middle of December
to continue on to Bodh Gaya, my next destination.
Though in size little more than a village in the impoverished state of Bihar, north-central India, Bodh
Gaya attracts thousands of visitors every year. The
Shakyamuni or historical Buddha attained enlightenment there five hundred years before Christ's birth.
Today pilgrims fly, walk, and rattle on mule-drawn
carriages into the town of huts and monasteries to
pay homage to Wisdom and Compassion.

I had written a Buddhist Studies program associated with Antioch College located in Bodh Gaya to
see if any saints in the area might be able to make
use of my assistance for a month. The director,
Robert Pryor, faxed me from Bodh Gaya as soon as
he received my letter.

"There's a woman out here you've got to meet,"

he wrote enthusiastically. "Sister Jessi. She's just what you're after. Please come."

I went. The thrill of a Buddhist pilgrimage spiced with the holiness of a Catholic nun seduced me immediately. My time there would be India, fully eclectic and paradoxical.

Sister Jessi wrapped her brown robes around herself and pulled socks on. Hobbling outside with the heels of her sandals crumpled under her feet, she spread newspaper on the low mud stoop under the window and re-swaddled herself. She huddled up against the wall and folded into prayer, covering her face with one raised hand. Though far more stiffly, I joined her and gathered a new brown cotton blanket around myself.

"This is how we'll pray," she said quietly, still hidden behind the blanket. "I'll say a verse, whatever comes to me, and then you say one, until we fall naturally into silence."

"OK," I piped merrily, then blushed in the dark for my lack of reverence, and we both resettled. She shuffled and her neck extended out into the cold for just a moment. A very graceful profile, gentle against dusk. I wondered if in her routine of work and prayer she remembered that she was beautiful. Her silvering gray hair was knotted loosely and fell down her back. I turned back to God.

"O give thanks unto the Lord...," Her voice trailed and in the emptiness I understood that my turn had come.

"For I know the plans I have for you...," I quoted.

Someone knocked at the door and she hushed me.

"Be quiet and wait," she said to me, but I, confused, started to try to think of another scripture to answer hers. Her face poked out of the wrapped blanket like a jostled bat and she watched the door. Knocking came again, this time accompanied by a timid call.

"Didiji? Didiji!" The farmers called her 'Honored Sister'.

"Sometimes," she smiled, "when we call on God, the Lord comes to the door. Ask and ye shall receive..." She pulled her gowns together into a manageable handful and huffed off to the far side of the courtyard and the blue wooden door. I caught sight of her smile falling as she turned from me. "Blow out the candles in the window," she called back.

While reaching through the window bars to the oil lamp I heard a man's apologetic voice and the sound of kids running inside. Sister Jessi asked me to check for leftover flat rice and block sugar from the teachers' meeting that afternoon. I brought out a newspaper funneled to hold the rice with brown sugar chunks bouncing on top. The two children shied from me and cupped their hands to receive the treat only from Didiji. She laughed, unabashedly flattered at their favoritism, and I receded into the darkening doorway to watch. Jessi pulled out two stools and played absently with one child's hand as the other crawled up her father's chest. He talked on, smiling, looking up at me frequently with a tourist's curiosity, and Sister Jessi nodded and smiled, answering only yes to encourage him. She stood to reshuffle the stoop's spread papers and looked to me in the conversation's break.

"He comes here always to talk and never stops."

As she spoke the man leaned forward. English was a curiosity to him, and he seemed to feel honored to have it spoken in his company, as if he were included in a circle of sophisticates. He had no idea what Jessi said. "And I can't tell him we were praying because it would embarrass him badly. He lives over in the house across the way, the one we rent a room out of, and he's talking about the sewer smell, you know, that you smelled before."

"He seems very kind." I nodded to the man. He chuckled proudly at this incomprehensible mention. When I laughed in return, the children hid behind his legs, frightened.

In addressing me Jessi did not attempt to camouflage her irritation. "Very kind, and he won't stop talking. Could you start to fix some soup or something to eat so that he will understand we were about to take our dinner?"

I scooped a handful of the pounded flat rice and sugar for a snack and lit candles to cook. Chickpeas, tomatoes, potatoes, chilies, water, salt. Such constituted our daily winter fare. I heard the man rising and Sister Jessi rushed into the house. I laughed to think she was running away from her guests. I brought a light into the adjacent room.

"Can I help you with something?" I asked.

The children had followed her in and were tugging at her dress hem. "They always come because they know I have candy and so they want some. Here," and she popped a hard mint into my hand, then stepped back into the evening with the kids carrying her train. She turned and they swirled behind her, a kite and its tail, wrapping fully around and binding her legs with her skirts. She laughed and teased them, holding the bonbons out of reach and then handing one to each. The smaller begged for two but got a false scolding instead. Jessi gave the father one for his wife and himself, and one for their smallest daughter as well. He thanked her profusely and she helped them across the threshold, bidding them good-bye. She closed the big blue door behind them and fastened it with a chain as wide as my hand. She sat on the stoop to recollect the broken silence in which we had been praying.

"Come, let's pray again," she said and then bent at the waist to pull her sandals off. She reseated herself.

"But the soup's cooking and it'll be ready soon," I called out of the back room. My hunger had begun to give me a sizable headache and my belly growled.

"Just turn it off and you can go back to it later. Praying on a full stomach isn't so good." By the time I'd come outside, a candle burned in the barred window again, and Sister Jessi was fully cocooned in her blankets. Her little body rose and fell with the flame and cold. I huddled next to her.

"Let us just breathe," she mumbled, and I started to focus. My breath came in, it went out, my stomach went out, it went in. In, out, in—a professor of mine, David Schenck, had taught us simple meditation in an introductory philosophy course between sections on Plato and Kant. My mind coursed among the evening's visitors and began to jump back through memory. My eyes opened to see the moon grazing on the treetops, as solid as the thoughts I couldn't clear from my head.

Sister Jessi breathed beside me, rustled and arched

against the night. She sighed and her forehead bowed.

"Didiji?! Didiji?" From the door, a call again interrupted us.

She bent further forward, then opened her eyes to stare into the ground in front of her. At the next knock she went again to the blue door. A new voice, that of Xavier, whispered to her through the crack. Short and compact as a barrel, Xavier managed a team of masons employed by Jessi. He needed to speak with her about the construction plans for the new school building so that his men could continue work the next day. Xavier's family was Catholic and originally from Sister Jessi's native Kerala. They enjoyed each other's Malayalam, a language spoken faster than Bihari truckers drive.

He came in and greeted me as they walked back to the house. Sister Jessi encouraged me to go ahead with my dinner preparations and asked me to fix some chai for the three of us as well. Once prepared, they both wisely turned down my repeated offers of soup. I covered the dish and returned to finish mixing the tea, a combination of Lipton sachets, granulated sugar and dry milk. Ever failing to mix the right amounts, I strainedmy eyes in the dark, but could not see whether the tea was well stirred. Setting the mugs beside them I saw white film from the milk floating on the surface. They snickered and teased that I would make a poor wife, even in America, then begged off my efforts to restir the brew. Politely they sipped it and returned to planning.

Outside I drank my tea greedily, film and all, and guzzled down the soup as well. Aside from flat rice my belly had been empty all day. But despite my hunger, I had little room to complain. Occasionally I would bicycle out to more isolated villages with one of Sister Jessi's schoolteachers to see a school and to distribute blankets to widows and orphans. Often we would be offered a meal, usually served on a large green leaf piled high with rice and covered in thahl, a thick vegetable sauce. This single meal was far larger and richer than what most others in the region would have in a day. The disproportionate size of children's teeth to their facial structure and the general thinness of everyone witnessed to the area's impoverished diet. I was gluttonous, if happily so, with my kettle of chickpeas and tomatoes. I coughed on the chilies and sneezed from the hot broth and cold.

For a while I sat listening to Xavier and Sister Jessi chatter. No one could have that much to say about brick-box architecture, and I waited to resume our prayers. Despairing of the moon's rise, I stood and started to pace, half-heartedly practicing walking meditation, sometimes singing. The night was a thin blue that swam through the trees. Trucks pounding down the Grand Trunk Road from Delhi to Calcutta burned the shambly brick houses with their head-lights and then the evening cool covered us again, quiet and chilling. I waited for Sister Jessi.

When Xavier left, Sister Jessi busied herself with arranging woven cots and a curtain to separate one room from the next. I began washing up, rinsing the pots and straightening the kitchen. Their tea was almost untouched.

"Shall we pray, Sister?" I called from the kitchen. Pulling back the ragged curtain she had strung up,

I saw her unfolding wool blankets over a cot. She gathered a stack of magazines and cartoon books and piled them sloppily in a corner as she spoke.

"No, no. It's too late now. You should rest." Though her tone often exactly fit her role as an ascetic burdened with the tiresome work of an organization's manager, a maternal strength and gentleness would sometimes turn in her voice. Her vocation was care. "Yes, tomorrow I need for you to go to Nuckaloopah to pass out uniforms to the students. So sleep. We'll pray together again, don't worry."

We finished cleaning and she left me alone in the room she had prepared, moving into the kitchen to make her own bed. I pulled off my shoes and pulled on my stocking cap, the night having become considerably colder since I'd enjoyed dinner outside. With one blanket under me and two tucked mummy-like around me I lay on the rope-woven cot and stared up into the darkness. My breath moistened the edge of the blanket. Inhaling, the smell of old wool cut my nostrils. Then sleep quickly descended.

In the night I woke suddenly, so cold that even the muscles under my eyebrows seemed unable to twitch. The stars pierced through the window grill.

The night had awakened me, the night itself, the sky's seared blue paled by the passing moon's light, and the moon had left space in its wake for the stars to fight in the early morning sky. Silence covered everything, silence thicker than the air, as solid as earth or a building, like a mortar filling the emptiness between the stars and me. I lay frigid in the complete stillness until I remembered the bicycle trip to

Nuckaloopah that I'd begin in a few hours, and I slept again.

When I awoke I noticed that the stars had moved. New formations blared through the window. But this time a rustling had awakened me, not the night. The thought of rats scampered across the back of my thoughts, but as I shook off my grogginess I realized that the curtain separating Sister Jessi's room from mine was glowing orange, brown-orange. The movement came from her room, and by the shadows playing across her ceiling I knew that she was awake, sitting on her cot and leaning over the light. Then I heard a soft sound rising.

She chanted, slow and under her breath. She had picked up the prayer left unfinished from our interrupted evening. I could not make out her words but the lower sounds came, clear from her throat, and at each word's beginning I could hear the saliva on her lips part. I listened to her, not to her prayer. The curtain shifted in the first morning draft from my window.

This was real devotion, and I was moved. No one watched her and she could not know of my observation. Sister Jessi frequently spoke about saints and virtuousness, and at times her whispered prayers to Jesus seemed spoken loudly enough for the benefit of my hearing as well as Heaven's. Sometimes her talk about fasting and humility bordered on egotism. The people of Bodh Gaya and its surrounding villages saw her as a holy woman, and she enjoyed that image. Religious sainthood was what she sought, and the strength of her desire had brought her to the conviction that she had to serve the less fortunate. Through their desperation the poor in Bihar called her and she had come, solely in search of God.

That morning as I prepared to leave for Nucka-loopah, Xavier knocked on the door. He greeted me in hesitant English.

"What you do for Christmas?" he asked.

"I don't know," I said and mentioned that Sister Jessi and I had briefly talked about my spending the time with her, joining in her devotions. He asked to see Jessi and spoke to her briefly in Malayalam.

"He is inviting you to go with him to Jarangdih, to his home for Christmas," she translated. Her eyes shifted to gaze at the trees across the road as we spoke. "He thinks you would enjoy spending Christmas with a family."

"I told him I might stay with you," I replied.

"You know Jarangdih, it's a coal-mining town in the south, in the mountains. And there are many Christians there."

"Yes," I answered. "I met two priests and some sisters in Delhi from south Bihar and they talked about it some."

"And there will be tea and cake, and dancing after the mass." She sounded like a tour guide half-heartedly selling me a travel package. "And lots of music. So maybe you should go. You're young and you'll enjoy being with those people, right?" Her look was incredulous, as if she could not believe that some people would actually enjoy a holiday party.

"Why don't you go with us?" I tempted.

"Oh, you know...me," she shrugged. The careless-ness of her tone could have been meant to communi-cate saintly detachment, but I also read in it the trumped up reasoning of a child afraid to join the group and needing some way to justify herself.

And so I spent that Christmas with Xavier's family, my contemplative desire bested by my curiosity and love of a Christmas with lights. Sister Jessi stayed behind to fast and pray the night on into the day, preferring solitude to the early morning dancing after Midnight Mass. And so I never prayed with Sister Jessi alone, though she before all other acquaintances that year most whetted my desire for a contemplative center in my life. Once one has attained silence of the heart, there is no need for silence around us, she would say. She aroused in me the hunger for action directed through prayer.

That morning she did not wake me. Without formal prayers I rose to her murmurs in the next room and went out into the morning, stripping off my shirt and sticking my head under a spigot. As I pumped, the cold water in late December rinsed me and shot my head empty for a moment. That is what prayer should be like—a moment of clarity that warms into benevolence. I pulled my shirt back on, wrapped a blanket about me, and went back inside smiling to fix our morning tea. I watched to see the powder dissolve completely.

I bicycled out to the small village called Nucka-loopah in order to visit the school established there by Sister Jessi and to assist in the distribution of the students' uniforms. Basudev, one of the original teachers of the program, and a few others went as well. They laughed as transport trucks bound down the Grand Trunk Road frightened me off onto the steep shoulder. My whole body jittered with the bike's rigid frame as I fought to keep pace. Soon we turned off the main road and started out over sunken fields, following a path that threatened to disappear under all of us at any moment.

As we wound through one village and passed to another, people would call out and laugh as we tried to avoid huge piles of cow dung and children. Weathered women threshing rice wheat stopped their work to wave and jeer at us. Everyone knew everyone and enjoyed that familiarity.

Upon reaching Nuckaloopah we dismounted and walked our bikes through a crowd out past their homes. A huge bodhi tree rose up after the huts and we stopped under it, leaning our bikes against a low building, pale blue. Basudevji explained that this was the village's temple, and the tree its school. He called the children into line.

Shy, but pushed forward by their grinning parents, the school's student body began to form under the tree's shade. Sisters pulled siblings into place according to height. The oldest boys remained aloof in the back file. One girl, crippled by polio, dragged herself smiling through the dirt to her place.

As Basudev began to speak a blind man lurched forward with a skinny boy riding his back, calling directions. The man stopped and eased the boy down to the ground. His spindly legs collapsed underneath him and two older boys ran up, lifted him on their shoulders, and brought him to position in the line. Basudev spoke again.

"This is a visitor," he explained, "a visitor of Mahisi Gyanodaya Abhiyan…of our school. He is a friend of

Sister Jessi and he is here to teach us and to visit us. He is here to bring you your uniforms." The crowd clapped, and a man ran out with two folding lawn chairs and a stool. We sat facing the children with their blue uniforms and white blouses stacked around us in the dust. Basudev leaned towards me and explained what he'd announced. "They want to sing you their welcoming song," he said.

The children stepped forward and grinned back at me. Feeling that some sign of respect was in order, I stood but felt exposed, the center of unexpected adoration. More than one soul between the Delhi airport and Nuckaloopah had explained to me that guests in India are considered as emissaries from God and are treated as such. But here I felt as if a work was expected of me, some kind of miracle to prove that these few congregated around dry fields and dung-mud huts were not forgotten. And in some way I did love these people who welcomed me so unabashedly. My smile was real. But my fumbling hands could only find my shirttail to pull on.

The children began to sing, a few beating their fists in cupped palms to stabilize the falsetto lilt. I rocked to the song's rhythm, not understanding its meaning, nervous and happy. And as I listened, I started to hear one word repeated at the tail of every stanza, just before a breath's break—"Didiji". I looked down at the teachers, two seated and one squatting on the ground. They looked not at me but smiled at their students and at the bodhi tree stooping over us.

I understood. This had nothing to do with me. I was welcome in the name of God's real representative, Sister Jessi. 'Didi', who is their sister; '—ji', who is to be most highly respected, as with 'Gandhiji'. She was being welcomed here in my person. My hands relaxed, I cupped my palm and clapped to join the boys' rhythm. The teachers ribbed each other and one took up the beat as well. We were not under the bodhi tree for my sake. We were there to celebrate Sister Jessi's advent.

Sister Jessi, to her family's chagrin, spent the majority of her adult life in convents and ashrams. Focusing first on Christian devotional prayer and then on Hindu-taught vipassanna meditation, she would spend years in unbroken silence. People would come to her requesting prayer and she would query and reassure them by writing messages on a chalkboard tablet. Her desire was a love of God so complete that she would be lost in undifferentiated divinity, egoless and burning.

Then she began to read newspaper articles about Bihar. The poorest province in India, the north-central state of Bihar has a government so corrupt that no one knows who holds the power anymore. Land seizures occur frequently both by those claiming government authority and also those unashamedly criminal. Bandits, called dacoits, raid buses and bull-drawn rickshaws between villages and especially around Bodh Gaya, a major international pilgrimage center for Buddhists wishing to pay homage to the site of the historical Buddha's enlightenment. Though markedly diminished in strength in other Indian states, Bihar still suffers from caste violence. In manner not terribly unlike hate crimes in the West, bands of upper-caste youth will destroy entire villages of untouchables simply because they believe themselves to have the right.

Mahatma Gandhi called these untouchables harijans, 'children of God'. Today they consider that name patronizing and instead call themselves dalits, meaning "oppressed". Fifty years ago, if a higher caste member passed through the shadow of a dalit while walking in the street, he was considered contaminated and had to be ritually cleansed. Though this is no longer the case today, other forms of discrimination still exist.

From an ashram in the Himalayas Sister Jessi read about the plight of dalit children. All Indian children legally enjoy the right to attend school. However, most lower-caste rural children must assist their parents with work in the fields. If one week they attend classes, the next requires them to be at home, and the pattern continues until they are irremediably behind in their studies and simply must quit. The system in Bihar is designed to hold the poor in place despite legal appearances of equality.

Sister Jessi left her ashram and her silence. Abandoning the Himalayas she went down into the Ganges Plain, south of the holy river, south of Varanasi and Patna, to the flat lands around the hill of Bodh Gaya. She began to visit villages of untouchables, calling the adults to school.

She taught illiterate and unmathed farmers basic reading, writing and arithmetic in order for them to assume the responsibility of teaching their own children. She then began to organize classes in villages. The teachers hold class in the mornings and students join their families to work in the afternoons. To augment discipline and the quality of instruction, Sister

Jessi asked nuns from south Bihar to work in her schools. Christians sometimes receive an advantage in education in Bihar because preferential placement is often given to them in Catholic classrooms, which are organized throughout the state. Sister Jessi and the schooled nuns educate the teachers, who in turn share their knowledge with their village's children. A network of 40 teachers, most instructing in more than one village, in schools ranging over a 20-kilometer radius has been established.

The grassroots school system is called Mahisi Gyanoday Abhiyan, the 'Campaign for Awakening Wisdom'. The addition of 'Messiah' to the name illustrates Sister Jessi's ambivalence about her religious loyalties. "Jesus is my guru," she repeated to me, along with her concern that others would see her simply as a spiritual seeker and renouncer of ties to the world in the Hindu sannyasin tradition and not as a Christian. "But," she says, "we're all after the same hope anyway, aren't we?"

The hope of the system does not target university enrollment for its students. Such advanced education is a cherished rarity for anyone in India, even for the wealthiest and highest castes. Aside from rudimentary school skills, students learn folk songs and dances and design practical dramas to teach youth how to confront a dacoit if one attacks her family or how to apply first-aid to a hoe-cut. They function as cultural centers meant to empower the minds of the youth rather than as ladders to assist them in social mobility.

When I arrived in Bodh Gaya to work with Sister Jessi in December 1998, the school term was ending. Exams were finished and students were being informed of their progress. To celebrate the winter term, cultural events were being held so that classes could share their projects with other students. One afternoon after delivering blankets on behalf of the school to widows in a village, Anand, Sister Jessi's scooter driver, and I zipped to an abandoned building where children and some parents had gathered. A group of girls clothed in their best saris, yellow and green and red, danced a traditional water dance, balancing invisible jugs on their shoulders and heads, dipping to gather water and turning gracefully for home. No better illustration of Rabindranath Tagore's love poems, in which a young man falls in love with a woman as she collects water, could be offered. They were followed by cheers and a drama of a holy person who converts a dacoit from a life of violence to one of peace and helpful service.

I sat on the building's far steps watching, laughing with the teachers and parents, trying to gather what each skit wanted to communicate. Here a boy rode out backwards on a sheet pulled over two of his friends, then dismounted and helped a wounded traveler onto the blanket; the Good Samaritan had come to a stranger's rescue with the help of his trusted mule. Now a tree wandered about with a boy, talking to him. It threw clothes out from its foliage and handed him more lemons than could be held. In the end the tree lay on top of the boy, all to illus-trate the benefits provided by the natural world—clothing, food, shelter—and the importance of living ecologically conscious lives.

The skits continued and the crowd grew restless. Older kids began popping younger ones in the ear and some ran off crying. The afternoon grew colder, and we shifted to sit in the sunlight.

In the midst of all this, a man stood up and walked stiffly before us. His dhoti lagged between his legs, puckering in the wind. With a scraggly white beard and ridiculous-looking yellow woolen cap he looked a bit like Santa after a long winter's nap. A squat little man, he gazed with hard tenderness at us, just standing, intent. And then he sang.

His voice was not so good, very gravelly and strained—perfect for his zeal. This man, whom previously I had watched having to deeply concentrate just to correctly write students' names, who had committed himself to these children, sang a song that he had fashioned for them.

Mother, what song is there to sing?
What water-fetching song for the morning?
Yesterday I sang only tears,
watching the others laughing.
Where were they going, running?
I have never seen a school.

Mother, what song is there to sing?
What sweet milk song for the morning?
Yesterday I sang only shame
Feeling the weight of a book.
What lights the eyes of others
Is heavy meaninglessness to me.

Mother, what song is there to sing?
I have no other song but joy.
This is the morning when the teachers came,

Calling me from sleep, calling me after chores—
Today I will hold a book in my mind,
Today I will write my name
One thousand times on every wall!

And it is true that on some walls in Nuckaloopah, Dhobi, and on towards Dumahane, scribbled names in scratchy Hindi script cluster between faded paintings of handprints and sprouting seeds.

For all the praise sung to Sister Jessi, she continues her work unsated. When Anand, who operates the school's sole vehicle, a motorcycle, scoots in late with alcohol on his breath she becomes infuriated and threatens his job, a more than reasonable reprimand for a driver. Teachers appearing hours late for meetings are harshly scolded. They do not argue and unhesitatingly admit their tardiness despite the universally accepted fluidity of time and schedule throughout India. These peasants, she told me, have no concept of time or responsibility. You have to really keep after them, or they'll all become lazy and do nothing worthwhile. In having me join the teachers for errands, she charged me with the money for fear that they would keep some of the change or purchase goods for themselves. She insinuated that others had lost their jobs already because of those kinds of deceit. A separation existed between the farmers and Sister Jessi despite their solidarity in the school's work.

But she sometimes provoked friction between people by not holding to her original plan or failing to prepare for an upcoming project. Once when some blankets needed to be purchased and distributed, she ran to her purse box, afraid that some teachers would discover where she kept the money hidden. She hadn't yet counted the money, and the mounting pressure of passing time and the arrival of everyone involved in the trip distracted her. Her count became confused and had to be restarted three times, her frustration and suspicion mounting the whole while. Finally the money was transferred and we left, only to arrive with insufficient funds to purchase the number of blankets she'd wanted. We pooled what cash we had and distributed the blankets. But upon hearing the story she became terribly embarrassed. She was hurt to have erred and to have forced the teacher-farmers to spend their own money, if only for a few hours, before they could be reimbursed. She took pride in helping them, knew embarrassment when she failed them, and railed at them when lateness or confusion prevented her from doing what she under-stood needed to be done for them, even if they were the cause of the obstacle.

When we were trying to sort uniforms and leave to distribute them, with people everywhere but where they should have been, she turned to me to vent her frustration.

"The thing I really wish," she muttered, "is that somebody like you would just come live here and handle all these problems. You could manage the money, you could buy the uniforms and sort them by size, you could bicycle to supervise the schools and teach some too. Wouldn't that be good? And then I could stay behind the work in prayer, supporting all that must be done with fasting and encouragement.

I could remain here in silence, that is what I do well. This managing I foul up always. But you see I am the one here who must do it now..." She walked off to straighten things out, and I stood wondering if there was anything to do then to remedy the situation. But without Hindi or the mind to comprehend Sister Jessi's erratic movements, I questioned anyone's aptitude to effectively help.

Solitude is more than holing up in seclusion to focus on the interior life. Sister Jessi walks a singular path and knows frustration in her much beloved religion just as she does in her work. Soon after my return from Christmas with Xavier's family in southern Jaranghdi, Sister Jessi asked how I wanted to observe the Sunday Sabbath. We could either stay in Dohbi at her office that doubled as a house, or we could join a small congregation of nuns at a little chapel in Dumahane. Curious about the unknown, I opted for the latter, and she began to apologize. "Maybe I'll just help you get on the bus and stay here myself. So hard for me to get up into the bus because of my knee, yes, you know, and that's why Anand drives me on the scooter. But he's at home still celebrating the holy day with his family and there is no telephone to call him."

"Wouldn't you come with me?" I asked. "You spent Christmas here fasting alone, you could join the sisters in Mass."

"Yes, but, you know, they like all those songs and celebrations, they like being together. That's why they live there together. But I like it quiet and without people telling me what I should do with the Buddhists and so forth. After all, we're all after the same hope, aren't we? And sometimes they don't think as I do…"

But on Sunday morning I saw Sister Jessi through the water I pumped over my head. She teased me about hurrying up and we scrambled up an embankment to the Gaya road. Mist lagged around us like cobwebs. It was cold; my breath curled up into the low clouds. I flagged a bus and we jumped on. With the conductor's help I hoisted her up, even with her bad knee, and the bus pulled away. She curled up in the seat and covered her face with her robe.

"Jesus," she began to murmur repetitively. The name disappeared into saffron swathing and the bus's brakes.

I helped her off at the Dumahane intersection, and we walked through trees down to a long walled gate. Stooping inside I smiled with delight. It was still Christmas. Streamers fled back across a long yard over marigolds and sunflowers to the convent's porch. Everything stood quietly as if abandoned and Sister Jessi trailed behind me as I stepped around the house. A little woman appeared in the doorway clothed in white.

"Oh, Sister Jessi and the American! We hoped you'd be here for Christmas. Good Christmas!"

"Yes, Merry Christmas, good Christmas," she smiled forcedly and walked into the house.

A little chapel welcomed us. Within we each took a place. Sister Jessi sat in what was apparently her regular seat in the right corner and the sisters gathered in front of her. Father Sumít, a Jesuit from the Bihari capital of Patna teaching ecology in Bodh Gayan schools, pulled off his motorcycle jacket and gloves and washed his hands. Walking into the white room, he squatted behind the low altar and wrapped a white cloth with orange edging around him as a chasuble. A woman entered and seated herself just to the altar's right. The door closed. We seven sat together. The room quieted and relaxed. Father Sumít opened the book of liturgy.

"Welcome, beloved, and good Christmas." From across the altar I smelled his hands, grained with motorcycle oil, bread and wine. He moved so intimately with the candles, I thought he might ignite.

The laywoman began to pound her fist in her cupped palm and sang. The sisters followed. Pulling out of his absorption with the book, the priest joined them and broke his austerity with a smile. Only Sister Jessi and I remained outside, I mumbling half-sounds of what Hindi my tongue could hold, Sister Jessi with her hand high over her face. She remained so throughout the Mass.

The room, so small and white, held us inside together against the outside cold. After the service the sisters asked that we stay for coffee and Christmas cake. "You stay," Sister Jessi deferred, "you'll enjoy it, won't you?" Without breakfast and happy in their company, I was more than willing. But her encouragement was less concern for me and more of an excuse for her. She hopped out into the garden and waddled to the gate. I chased after her.

"Wait, Sister—are you sure it's all right for me to stay? I can come back with you now. It'll be no bother at all. Look, don't you need a hand to get into the bus?"

But she chuckled and nudged me off, insisting that

the fare collector would help her and that she'd meet me back in Bodh Gaya at the Burmese Vihara, our second home. She scurried out along the road towards the Dumahane crossing and I went back for coffee.

"I never understand her," one of the sisters pecked. "Always we invite her to come to Mass, and then if she comes she won't even stay for tea and coffee."

Father Sumít shrugged and dipped a cookie. "Maybe she doesn't like coffee so well." The sisters laughed. "Or maybe she doesn't like all of us!" One quieter sister almost spit her tea, she found the joke so hilarious.

After the snack Father Sumít offered me a ride into Bodh Gaya on his motorcycle. As we pulled out onto the main road he called back to me. "Sister Jessi, you know, I respect her very much. The work that she does, no one else can do it. And such an austere lifestyle, and such gentleness. But I wonder if she gets lonely sometimes, out in that brick office and quiet all the time. She could come to Mass more often." His musing fell off into the motor's drone and dropped into Bodh Gaya's caked plain.

During my brief two months in India, newspapers reported nationwide attacks on Christians by militant Hindu groups almost everyday. Christmas time provided a politically auspicious season for the central culprit, the Vishwa Hindu Parishad, thought by many to be the strong arm of the majority Bharatiya Janata Party, to provoke divisions between Hindus and

Christians. The main trouble occurred in south Gujarat, a western state to which I would go in January. Sister Jessi teased me maliciously about the understood question of whether or not I should go. "Maybe they'll…," she joshed, pulling her finger across her throat. She giggled and went in to fix tea.

I first went to Dohbi from Bodh Gaya to meet Sister Jessi's teachers. With presents of plaid scarves and tin cups crammed in my pockets, I clambered up top a rickety bus and braced for the half hour, 24-kilometer ride out to her home. She'd arranged a Christmas celebration for the teachers that coincided fortuitously with my arrival.

When I had arrived the first night in Dohbi, a street vendor showed me the path down to Sister Jessi's building. Half the space consisted of five low rooms that opened onto a dirt courtyard. A rough brick wall embraced the area. Teachers were crawling along the roof and walls hoisting a tarp over two-thirds of the inner yard, and one leaned over the edge to hang a paper-maché star. They stood and laughed a greeting at me. I laughed back, and then everyone froze—we'd gotten as far as we could saying hello and suddenly found ourselves stuck. Everyone stared oddly at each other, not ill at ease but nonetheless lost.

"Hey, what's all this, haven't you got it hung yet?" Sister Jessi fussed in English as she tumbled through the big blue door from outside. "Oh, you're here," she cried, almost happily, as if she'd just seen me. "I wondered what had taken you so long. Did you get the bus all right? How much did you pay? That's good, not too much, OK. Come, I've got something for you to do."

We went off to wrap presents for everyone, hand towels, handkerchiefs, mugs, and pens, and returned after dark. Outside the building men clustered, stoking a fire on which a big dented kettle nestled. They huddled, keeping warm against the night. Just inside the blue door on another little hearth, subjee, a dish of vegetables, stewed.

Sister Jessi scolded everyone mildly for being so late and for having started the cooking after dark. "Some of you will have to stay with the fires and miss the Christmas gathering," she menaced, and the group laughed sheepishly. Woolen blankets were spread under the tarp and we folded ourselves into squatting rows, the women in front. I went to the back to hide and watched the stars pass through tears in the blue plastic.

"This Christmas gathering is to explain what Christmas is about," Sister Jessi began, addressing the seated group. "Here you see a little house of hay and some paper animals and people. Some of the teachers, Sisters Mary and Teresa, and Anand, built it to show you the story." A rude crèche wobbled on the mud stoop before us like an altar setting. One sister stood up and recited an explanation of Christmas. Her eyes stayed stapled to the ground, head bowed.

"Thank you, very good. Um, Scott?—maybe you could come up and tell us what Christmas means to you, what it means to be a Christian. Come, come up here." She shooed some people back with her foot to make space for me to stand.

"I don't know if I ever understood what it means to be a Christian until a little while ago," I began.

Sister Jessi rattled off her Hindi translation. "I was in Thailand, to the east, working in a hospital with people dying of AIDS—"

"*I don't think they'll know what AIDS means,*" she hissed, then turned back to the crowd and somehow improvised. "OK, I told them 'very sick people'. Go on."

"So, working with these people, I tended one particular man everyday. His name was Jarune." And I continued the story of Jarune, of Prichya coming out of the tuberculosis ward and calling to me about a hand, my hand, the hand of God caring for Jarune. The congregation sighed en masse. "Being a Christian," I ended, "simply means asking God to live in you."

"Thank you, yes, thank you. That is right," Sister Jessi murmured, her voice trailing thoughtfully. Never would I hear her speak with such a reflective tone as in those few words. She quickly recovered.

"OK, thank you, and now we will give some presents. We have tonight with us a very famous person in the world, he brings lots of things, presents, and happiness to boys and girls all over the world if they are good. And he is here tonight to bring something to the good teachers of our school, Mahisi Gyanoday Abhiyan." The parental condescension in her voice had begun to lose its cuteness and was becoming mildly obnoxious to me. But the teachers looked as happy as kindergartners just before their midmorning Kool-Aid is served. "Baba Christmas? Come, come!"

From the dark doorway behind her, Father Christmas leapt out. His long white beard fell in tangles of cotton swabbing and glue. His shoulders were draped in the most elegant of green shawls. Dingy brown pants disappeared in the shadows beneath the stoop's candles. Wrapped in red bands of wool, his head sprouted white cotton locks. Hay thrust out of his pants' hem like misplaced antlers. He bent over the crowd as if to tickle us and a shouted laugh caught in his beard, falling muffled on the ground. He grabbed the first present and prepared to call out the name. But his lips stumbled, half-open.

"*Dande,*" Sister Jessi whispered, and the letters came together.

"Dande," he hollered and leapt at Dande who surged forward himself. They hugged each other and bounced up and down for a moment. Then Baba Christmas pressed a paper-wrapped metal cup into Dande's hand. He held it high for everyone to see and a silly-hearted cheer went up. The men poked at Dande as he went back, teasing him with hugs and slaps.

"Basudev!" This he could read and so called it out resoundingly. Basudev left off his teasing of Dande and solemnly processed to the front, stumbling over every row. Baba Christmas threw himself around Basudev's neck and wrung him into smiles.

Sister Jessi couldn't feed Santa presents fast enough. I in turn skipped up for my prize and found two presents in my hand and beard cotton from a hug in my mouth. Before I returned to my seat, the sisters began to sing.

Everyone quieted and a natural reverence blended with the late night to calm us. The teachers listened to gain their colleagues' words; I understood the heart of the song and listened to the melody, slow and somber, much like "O Come, O Come Emmanuel," but with a wailing harmony behind the song's screen. The stars in the sky looked down where we sang. Sister Jessi had seated herself on the ground with us, and after the carol she started a chant. Basudev rocked in her rhythm, echoing the verses. Others picked up the next stanza with him, until all the teachers voiced prayer. We had gone from celebration to celebration, from gifts to prayer. We stilled into the responsory's ending.

Suddenly Basudev croaked out, "Jai Ram, Jai Ram, Jai Jai Ram!" but we failed to second the line and he tried to recover, his voice breaking self-consciously.

"Jai Ram, Jai Ram, Jai Jai Ram!"

"Praise God, Praise God, Praise, praise God!" One of the front women echoed him, and after his next call the group sang in one voice.

"Jai Ram Jai Ram Jai Jai Ram!"

Someone began singing along with the chant and we moved into a song. Hands clapped and people started to rock in their seats. I leaned back and listened, watching Sister Jessi rock and sing in chorus. The fire-tenders poked in through the blue door and slipped off cackling, back to the rice. Over us the sky listened with the neighbors across the field. Later we would eat rice and subjee, and afterwards Sister Jessi would curtain off her back room. Lighting a candle, she sat through the night murmuring these same chants, indiscriminate of origin, intent on their tone and object more than their words.

For then she sat with her teachers, Hindu and Christian.

The Saints

When I first arrived in Patna, I had three free days
in my hands. At the end of that time I would meet
Sister Jessi, but for the moment I could do anything,
go anywhere. India was fresh and my naiveté liberat-
ing. Everything was possible. But on my first dusty
morning I wandered into the care of an old Jesuit
missionary, Father Kanealy.

In trying to find the Ganges I spotted a church
steeple and decided to enter the chapel to collect
myself before going on. I hadn't crossed half of the
churchyard before a man walked up to me. He wore a
faded green jacket and Converse All-Stars that looked
like he'd played ball in them since the '50s.

Sizing me up, he spoke. I could only look back
at him. "I'm sorry," I answered stupidly. "I don't speak
Hindi."

With a wry smile and a Chicago accent the man
replied, "You're not from around here, are you?" He
invited me into the building adjoining the church.

After fixing me coffee and eggs for breakfast,
Father Kanealy spent the next three days zipping
me through Patna on the back of his motorcycle. He
showed more vigor than any other 73 year-old I had
ever known, jumping up on tables to change light
bulbs and joyriding the new Indira Gandhi Bridge
as evening fell to night. Introducing me as "Scott
Neely, my long-lost nephew," he took me to as many
Catholic and social service organizations as we could
fit into those days.

On a walk one morning we detoured to see a
residential section of town. The neighborhood was
an archetypal city slum. Kids played half-naked in

clusters; mothers bent over clay stoves on the side-walks; sluggish streams of waste drained down the street. Constructed of cardboard and plastic sheeting fastened together with sticks, the shelters resembled precariously perched dominoes. I looked to Father Kanealy. He was smiling.

"Look," he said in wonder. "Aren't these people amazing? They keep their families warm in the winter and dry when the rains come. Aren't they amazing?"

His admiration was real, not at all trumped up praise to give a squalid life dignity. Then he said something stunning.

"You know," he said out of a side-ways grin without looking at me. "Jesus died for all of these people, and most of them don't even know it."

Not a trace of sadness could be found in his voice. At my age fifty years ago he had left the United States to work as a missionary and as a teacher among the poor in Patna. And here he seemed to admit his own vocational defeat without disillusionment.

Somewhere along the way he learned to love rather than to control. He was not the one that made people what they were, whether Hindu, Muslim or Christian. Somehow, maybe simply by living among them and serving them, he had learned to see something in them that surpassed the work of conversion, something innate.

He had not compromised his calling. His life and words testified to his belief. He was able to love perfectly, without equivocation. Love beyond religious logic had brought him to happiness.

Jamnagar, Gujarat, India

21 January - 28 February 1999

In our father's house
I found you,

Adolescent, wanting
The perfection you knew was possible.

I committed the error of traveling by plane within India. The flights were never miserable or even extremely tardy, although delays were frequent. Service was always warmly courteous with a comforting mix of English correctness and Indian grace. Aside from one landing—in Patna in December—danger never crossed my mind.

Coming over the widening silver sliver of the Ganges in mid-afternoon, the plane touched down and began rolling across the runway. But the pilot failed to put the front wheel down and for a long time we sped past scraggly grass and people lounging in the air strip fields, brakeless. The few seconds during which this continued seemed long in our minds, and a growing awareness of trouble crescendoed as the frame of the plane began to rattle. Suddenly the nose dropped, the front wheel bounced and skidded as the pilot threw on the brakes, and we fishtailed our way to a halt. The cabin erupted into thunderous applause, but one begrudging member of the audience muttered in the seat behind me, "That's not funny, that's not funny at all! It's really dangerous! What the hell did he think he was doing, not putting the brake-foot down…?!" His fiancée soothed him, reminded him to be thankful that he was still alive, and told him he would get used to being back in the country soon enough.

My mistake in flying did not concern logistics. The problem was with isolation. When traveling in a country that could rightly be divided into autonomous bodies by state just on the basis of population and cultural difference, flying threatens to blur the perception of what India is. If one attempts to understand a people, giving time to the elite has its value. But few Indians have seen an airplane, much less been inside one. To fly is to remove oneself from the general throng of the country. Even only a short train ride should be required in any wanderer's itinerary so that one might understand how the majority of Indians travel, packed in a box car circus for an indefinite number of hours. But the proletariat cannot teach everything about a civilization.

The isolation constructed by a plane is less cultural than geographic. The argument is old but valid. Jumping on a plane in Patna and hopping off in the western state of Gujarat means missing the slur of dialects and cultures that a train ride can reveal. Flight over the Ganges may sometimes mean ecstatic views of the distant Himalayas, but more often than not one hovers over a humid blur of undefined plain for about

three hours. The rising of Uttar Pradesh out of flat
central Bihar, the turning of Rajastan into Gujarat—
I can only imagine what is missed, as I know only the
missing. But the body of the country and the passage
through its people I regret having forgone.

En route to Jamnagar, a port city in the western
coastal state of Gujarat, my flight lay over in Mumbai,
once Bombay. The humidity of the city knotted my
clothing around my chest and between my legs as
I wandered back and forth across parking lots trying
to find the domestic check-in station. Streetlights
blurred in the thick air. It was late. Passed from hand
to hand and mouth to mouth with advice, I came at
last into the waiting area for the next day's flights.

A dark purple cordon sliced the room in two,
separating the entrance and the waiting seats from
the check-in area. On the left, stretched between
chairs with nothing supporting their waists, men
slept. Beneath one a woman lay curled in her sari,
a blanket wrapped from her forearm around her back
and hooked beneath her hips. Her legs splayed languidly on the linoleum. Across the hall on the right
the matriarchs of a family bickered loudly. A team of
moppers interceded to ask them to move their legs
a little. A shift, and the argument resumed. The male
janitors wore rumpled monkey suits and spoke little.
Their skin was notably darker than that of everyone
else in the room. With them worked women in saris,
muscling their mops down the floor and then back
in the other direction. They spoke quietly to one
another on rare occasions and never raised their
heads to meet anyone except when I tried to enter
the bathroom while they were still working. 'Just

wait,' they motioned dully, and I did. I returned to a removed spot under a row of seats that I'd chosen and rewrapped myself in my thin beige blanket.

Lying there I listened to the lights hum. The humidity filled the empty pockets between the blanket and myself, and occasionally I'd flap it open for ventilation. The family of women argued, the scrubbing of the maintenance staff continued steadily and low. I slept, woke, went to the bathroom, slept hard again.

There was a peace in that night. After weeks I had finally found a phone on which to speak with my mother, albeit for maybe three minutes. I was alive still, safe and content, and they now knew it. Another few weeks could pass with less anxiety on both sides of the globe.

And I felt soaked into the place. I was as transient as the rest. The dampness of the dark and the indifferent drudgery of the janitors accepted me as they did everyone else that night. I felt a part. During those hours, even in sleep, I understood that I was there, in Mumbai's domestic airport, and not coming or going anywhere.

In Jamnagar the next day a crowd swallowed us as we stepped off the plane and walked across the runway. Family engulfed the waiting area, all one undifferentiated family to my eyes, complete with handpainted signs welcoming the homesick husband or mother. I slipped through a side door to avoid the ruckus and unwittingly gave myself over to an even greater chaos.

As I emerged through the door I caught the eye of a rickshaw driver. He scrambled to me, holding me by the hand and insistently drawing me toward his vehicle. "100 rupees," he grinned at me, to which I answered, "50, 50." He smiled back in delighted deafness.

But he couldn't get me to his station fast enough. Before we had descended the entranceway porch twenty more drivers mobbed us, all trying to get their price in my ear. They could have been unionized, the number was so consistent.

"50," I argued to their litany of hundreds. I heard a '75' pop above the crowd and I looked at the man offering to see if we could agree.

Then from the side a hand snagged my shirt and snickered a mischievous "50? OK, 50?"

"Yes," I called even before I could turn to see the new driver. As I did, the crowd erupted, raining down insults on the new front runner. 'How could you betray us?' I imagined them shouting. Real anger screwed in the eyes of a skinny man just before us. My driver grabbed my wrist and pulled me across the packed sand parking lot into the shadow of his rickshaw. He was laughing as if I were his cohort.

"Najtampuri Dam, Khijada Mandir," I repeated, trying to make him understand the address of the temple I needed to reach. He rattled through the quiet city afternoon and I watched a new month spread around me.

Cows graze in my memory as the first marked element of Gujarat's identity. In Bihar the cows were thinner than the children. Bone eroded bone as they walked, thick sticks thumping their sides in the rice wheat fields and down streets. But in Jamnagar's cows, muscle showed instead of skeleton. Their coats shone sleek and white, fatted underneath. We passed a man, his head bound by a bright red and unraveling turban, feeding a bull green grass from his hand. The animal contemplated the hand and its city with low, intelligent eyes.

A teacher at the ashram in which I was going to live for the following month would later tell me that Gujarat was a moral state. Indians fear Bihar for its corruption, Kashmir for its beauty and violence; they love Rajastan for its history and architecture and Gujarat for Mahatma Gandhi and religion. "No one in Gujarat will mistreat the cows," he told me. "Some cow owners that have no way of feeding their animals simply let them wander in the streets. They know that someone will feed them during the day."

"Najtampuri Dam," I repeated. When questioned, a weightless little man on the road's shoulder pointed us down a side street, and we came quickly to the painted gates.

I stepped through the high sculpted doors of the temple compound and stood in the clean dirt plaza for a moment before being noticed. Men conferred in small clusters around the edges of buildings. The early afternoon shadows had begun to fall. Their white shirts and dhotis, thin cotton skirts, looked blue in the shade and some wore wool sweaters and toboggans. Dusty from the ride and scared about what to do next, I scanned the interior of the ashram. For a moment, the settling quiet and my wariness changed the space into a showdown scene from a Western.

"Hello, hello?" followed by something else I

couldn't catch came from behind me. I turned and saw a slight man, large nosed and about my age, reaching forward with friendly timidity to touch my arm.

The scattered groups around the courtyard perimeter now formed a full crowd around me. Everyone laughed and kept repeating something I couldn't understand. They seemed to be asking a single name and I assumed they meant to know either who I'd come to see or who had sent me. Having come to work with the spiritual director and manager of the temple, I began saying his name.

"Maharajshri. Maharajshri?" At this the laughing mounted, although some faces grew more serious. Groups were beginning to form again, undoubtedly around disagreements about who I was and what was to be done with me.

Those speaking to me kept repeating the same name as before. It occurred to me that they might be saying the name of my reference. The parents of one of my close school friends had immigrated to the United States from India. After hearing about my project, her mother had suggested I visit Khijada Mandir, a Pranami Krishna Temple. The temple is the Vatican, though on a significantly smaller scale, of a branch of Hinduism known as the Pranami Krishna sect. Followers are devotees of Krishna as a manifestation of the Godhead. They adhere to the teachings of the sect's seventeenth century founders, Dev Chandraji and Pranathji.

As the men kept repeating whatever it was they were saying I realized that I didn't know the first name of my friend's mother. I'd always referred to her as Mrs. Gandhi. If they were asking if I was the one she had sent, I wouldn't be able to recognize the question. So I began saying, "Teek, teek, yes, yes," when they spoke in the hope that my response was right. Surely something would come of giving a response, no matter how incorrect.

The crowd began to look flustered and one young man spun to run out the gate. Gently taking my arm another led me into a high blocky building and seated me in a cool foreroom. My guide received a glass from another and passed the water to me.

I was thirsty. I was flustered at not being able to communicate. Although having difficulty with language had by then become more of a game than a hindrance, I hadn't expected to run into it here. The exchange of faxes arranging my stay a few months previous had beenin good, even eloquent, English. Today was the decided day of my arrival. I'd anticipated spilling a few inept words on the pavement and quickly being ushered off to the resident English speakers. The frustration of my unwitting hosts bothered me; I felt myself a nuisance. I wanted a bath after two days traveling. I hadn't eaten much since the day before. Gujarat was proving much warmer than Bihar. A palm extended the water as a welcome and as something to occupy a few seconds that conversation certainly wouldn't fill.

Later it would be explained to me that all of the temple's water comes from the well around which many of the men were sitting when I first walked through the gates. That well formed when the founder of the sect, Pranathji, struck the ground with his hand. The source has fed the temple for centuries, and even during times of drought it has never run dry. Its quality has also never caused problems. I would drink from it daily during my stay without ever suffering illness.

But I did not know the water's mythology at the time. I could only think about thirst and the desire not to disrespect my hosts. Deciding it best to enjoy the moment even if it might doom the future, I drank.

Before I had finished the cup a heavy figure crossed the threshold and waddled into the room. A frog-faced man, bald but for fine wisps of white covering his skull, squinted at me crossly, then smiled. It was the smile of a self-known savior and not one of welcome. He greeted me with folded hands.

"I am Greesbhai. And you must be Mr. Scott Neely."

I bowed back and grinned largely. "Yes."

"You are early." He motioned for an attendant to position a chair across from me, in which he slowly situated himself.

"Early?" I was caught off guard. Today was the day agreed upon for my coming. The flight dates assured me that I had not made a mistake. Today was the planned day of arrival. "I'm sure today is the day we agreed upon. January 22nd, no?"

"Yes, and you should have come on the 28th. Your teacher expects you on the 28th and he will not be here until then. So that is almost a week." He spoke slowly, as if meditating on the precise articulation of every word. He gave the impression of being right.

"I am so sorry," I leaned forward. I started to offer to return in a week on the new day, explaining that I was there to help and that I certainly did not want to interfere with the flow of routine in the temple. I wanted to ask what teacher he was talking about but hardly had the chance. If I had come to Jamnagar by train instead of plane there would have been no problem with arriving early.

"No, no, that is fine, you may stay. In India, a guest is never refused, even if he is early or completely unexpected. Until your teacher comes, I will teach you. I taught in the high school for over fifty years, and still I am giving private lessons in my home. So I will be your teacher until Vishwanatji arrives from Mumbai. Now," and he paused to sip the hot chai that another young man had just slipped into the room. "You want to speak to Maharaji. He does not have much time for speaking to everyone, but you have arrived, and you are his guest, so he will gladly see you. He is a good Maharaj, much more liberal and open to thinking than the ones before." He hoisted himself up in his chair and gingerly held the cup again with his chubby fingers to drink. A few drops spilled brown down his white front without his noticing. "You see, I am not very religious. With this Maharajshri I can speak what I believe and come to the temple as I see fit. You see, I am a dialectical materialist. I have been a member of the Communist Party here since even before Independence. So in general I see little need for religion and its superstition." He pronounced his convictions as if presenting a dissertation. His pride extended far past his belly.

I had begun laughing at almost everything around me since my time in Thailand. Maybe Phra Phongthep had passed his mischievous contagion on to me, or perhaps I'd stopped trying to understand the general absurdity of the world and had begun instead to laugh with it. For whatever reason, I smirked again as Greesbhaiji spoke. Distracted and maybe annoyed, his discourse swayed for a moment. "No...," he began, but at that moment the man who had brought us tea returned to summon us. The Maharajshri was ready to see us.

"When he comes in," my new teacher instructed, "bow, and wait for him to speak."

We sat at an office table across from an empty rolling chair. Greesbhaiji watched it attentively, chin up, dignified, as if he had brought me into the room to present me. I touched my hair, mussed and needing a wash from the past days on planes and floors. Attendants waited silently along the walls. A few would stand still and then suddenly scurry out, returning after a few seconds. Then the opposite wall opened.

A man of great elegance and cleanliness stepped into the room. The wall had slid open without warning. Everyone bowed and Greesbhaiji rose slowly, bending his head over puffy folded hands. I grabbed the armrests of my chair and stood, trying at once to show respect correctly and to watch everyone else to know what to do. I hardly made it halfway up before it was time to sit again. I reseated myself hurriedly as the Maharajshri settled, spinning lightly in his swivel chair to face us. He placed two well-manicured hands flat on the tabletop and pulled himself forward.

He was extremely clean and, even more noticeably, clothed fully in shades of pink. Underneath his rose shroud he wore an orange-pink tunic and a darker sarong. A fuchsia pillbox hat crowned him. His hair fell long and straight in the back, jet black and brushed meticulously straight. He was kempt to such perfection that I fleetingly wondered if he bathed himself. The care he received had to border on pampering.

With a very unsure, quavering voice he addressed me.

"You are very welcome here."

"Thank you," I answered deferentially.

"Your teacher has been telephoned in Mumbai and will come as soon as he can. Until then Mr. Greesbhai will instruct you."

"Thank you," I said again. "I'm very sorry to cause trouble." Greesbhai smiled to himself.

"You will be wanting a bath. Basantaji is the temple manager here. He will show you to your room." A small and very handsome man, compact, hawk-nosed, nodded curtly in service. I nodded back at his propriety.

"So you are welcome. Now…is there anything else you would like to know about this Khijada Mandir or about me?" I thanked him but asked to wait for another time to question him. I would like to have an interview, but perhaps not yet. Still, there was one thing: When could I start working?

I had come to the temple to work in the free medical clinic run every day of the week. I wanted to watch the Maharajshri fulfilling his role of saint in service to the poor and sick. I had come to assist and to learn from his holiness.

"You will not work here," he said as if to reassure me. "You are a student from the United States, a scholar. That work is not for you. While you are here you must learn about us, about our religion. Then you can teach others about it in your own country."

The prospect of learning about Hinduism so intimately excited me greatly. But I had come to see engaged religion and not just to learn theology. He read the hesitation in my eyes.

"And maybe sometimes, if you have time, you can visit the doctor's clinic to see what we do. Helping is important, we do believe, but it is not the most important..." A phone rang and was brought into the room. The Maharajshri excused himself. Our meeting had ended. Holding onto my arm, Greesbhaiji walked with me into the expanding afternoon shadows.

When Vishwanatji, my appointed teacher, arrived a few days later, I was ready for him.

The first few days passed pleasurably in the ashram, slowly, a welcomed rest after Sister Jessi's scatteredness. But time grew heavy as it wore on. The Krishna murals along the temple interior began to turn cartoonish and could hold my interest for only so long. Prasad, the crushed sweets given to visitors in the temple as a blessing from the deity, seduces the most ascetic saint. After some days, however, the taste ripens and becomes too insistent, too pious and dry in the mouth, and I soon tired of eating it. The world inside the temple shone brightly, beautifully, when first met—the washed temple floor before dawn, cold and wet under foot; the putty-fat sculptures adorning the gate in flat, vivid colors. But I did not understand the content. On the first evening Basantaji gave me a few pamphlets in English about the history and theology of the denomination. Their simplicity could not sate the need I had for a fuller understanding of my context. The sweetness and brightness had meaning that I could not access. When I turned to those who knew they eagerly smiled, but only smiled, behind Hindi and Gujarati.

Unable to attain its secret I watched the temple move around me, walking its surface and waiting. I would come to lunch as soon as the bell rang but always found myself the last inside the cavernous kitchen. Already the residents of the ashram, all men and similar to Christian monks in their contemplative, priestly vocation, sat in two long facing rows along the left side of the floor. They must all have loitered by the door in wait for the signal to eat. Lunch was served at eleven as the day's first meal. Before dawn we would drop from our apartments into the freshly swabbed kitchen and take a cup of warm sugared milk, fresh from the temple's cowherd kept just outside the city. By midmorning hunger had us all.

A series of trough-like sinks separated the cross-legged men from an empty table and its attendant chair. Slipping off my sandals I stepped the thirty or so yards from the entrance to my place and sat. A novice was appointed each day to wait on me. It seemed to give immense pleasure to the young men of the ashram when they were chosen to scoop out my serving of subgee, a kind of vegetable stew eaten with rice or chapati, an unleavened bread. Twice a day, at lunch and dinner, I sat at table and watched the white-clad saints, as they were called, washing their dishes in the basins as I began to eat.

When I entered the temple, monks would hurry up to me and tenderly take my hand. Every escort wanted to show me the gnarled tree around which the main shrine stood, wanted me to touch the trunk where centuries of hands had rubbed it smooth, wanted me to see the trickling stream where their first holy man had brought water out of nothing but stone. They pulled me into their circle during hymns, urged me to pound something out on the miniature harpsichord passed from lap to lap, showed me when to bow to what and signed that what I was doing was very good, that the act was very holy. In between services they took me to their rooms, seated me on the few spare cushions, showed me the handful of books they kept or photographs of their homes in Nepal and Gujarat. They shone with delight that I had come into their chamber as a personal guest. We toured the four cracked walls, the high window. We sat on the floor. We smiled. We sputtered insubstantial politeness in English and Hindi. We looked at each other and joked a bit. The laughing subsided into quiet. I shifted my legs from the pain in my ankles. We were together, expectant, and nothing came.

A weight had begun to grow. It came from underneath the routine of the temple and its appearance, emerging slowly and subtly and then bearing down with increasing heaviness. I was waiting for something more, and so were they. I knew why I had come. All I needed was for the means of achieving it to arrive from Mumbai. The road had turned without notice, but I could get back to it.

But they did not understand. The coming of a U.S. American student to work in their clinic seemed inconceivable. To them I was a scholar from a wealthy world, not a worker. Besides, I had no medical skills and no language ability. They welcomed me and took great pleasure in serving me. But no one could understand why I was in their temple. I clearly had not come as a pilgrim like the other visitors in the compound.

During those first days Greesbhaiji would come mornings and afternoons to talk with me for an hour or so. We always met in the same room that served as a waiting area for the Maharaji's offices. It was cooler inside. With the doors open a draft would pull past us, and we could position our chairs in the sunlight if Greesbhaiji chilled. In the evenings when the mosquitoes came out all we had to do was shut the door. As long as one of the young monks brought in fresh cups of chai, Greesbhaiji could talk. History, culture, his religious convictions, nostalgia for Nehru's India, concern for the failings of government today—he told me what he thought in the same measured tones. He lectured but not in a professorial manner. The role of aged counselor suited him better and he assumed the part without hesitation. Though in my mind I often mocked him, his amity fed me during those days, and his pride gave me the wall I needed to push against. He kept my will from atrophying, and I felt justified in all my quiet resistance.

He would say, "Now. *Om* is a sound that you do not have in your English language." The edge in his voice set my defensive hairs on end, the way they stand when a non-South Carolinian starts to criticize my state. I can poor-mouth my region's foolishness into eternity, but my feet are also caked with red clay. "It is a letter and a sound in the ancient Sanskrit language, which preceded our Hindi of today, and was perfected by the sages of old." Veneration of the Indian scholar from Nehru back into antiquity dominated as a theme in these talks. "This sound *Om...* go on, try to say it."

"*Ahhmah,*" I opened my mouth.

"No no, *O-h-m...,*" he corrected. "You will feel that it touches your soul. In this word there is liberty. Now. *O-h-h-m...*"

"*Uhohmmh.*"

Genuinely insulted, he grimaced at my effort. He tilted back his head as if under the care of a dentist and dropped his lower jaw wide. "Like this." He looked down the slope of his backturned face to catch my eyes, then closed his own and groaned piously. "*Ooohhmmmmmm...*"

The resonant depth lost its focus as it dissipated into the room. He had found the word, free of all the hollowness and straining I had produced in the back of my throat when trying.

"*Om,*" I said quickly. He started and smiled. I had done it. I had said the word quickly enough with no prolongation on the final "m", and it had sounded near enough to correct to elicit a smile. Greesbhaiji resituated himself in his chair and mumbled something about the chai being cold.

"Hey!" he called to the door behind him. A shadow passed but no one entered. He tried to turn to see the entrance but couldn't move his mass. Leaning further back, he clapped his hands. No answer.

"Come," he said to me with some irritation. I stalled at the door for him to shuffle even with me, and we stepped into the courtyard. Waving at a few monks conversing earnestly in a corner, we walked through the gate and into the street. As we passed under the portal's shadow and our feet touched pavement he took my right arm firmly in his grip. Cars swerved down the narrow alley. A few stalls stood along the side, placed there in an attempt to snag straggling customers uninterested in the main market at the street's head. The vendors sat on a low stoop with their feet tucked tight against themselves, out of the way of bicycles and scooters. We walked up the low grade. Cows chewed grass and rags at their leisure. Without a word Greesbhaiji cast them an approving glance.

"They are very beautiful," I said, honestly taken but also fishing for his thoughts. He looked ahead and allowed his smile to open only slightly. "Their eyes are so graceful, like deer."

"Here we are," he motioned as we met the main street. He stepped heavily over a wide gutter running full to an overcrowded tea stand. Two men worked the business. One poured tiny glasses to the brim with steaming chai. He held two kettles at once, pouring with both hands and indicating with his elbows which glass was for which customer. Empty cups piled quickly on a warped board that functioned as a table. The speed with which cups were filled, finished and returned resembled a magic show in which both the audience and the magicians knew well their part. Everyone played the game deftly. The second worker at the stand grabbed two empty glasses at a time and flushed them with water, scrubbed them with his fingers and stationed them for a new fill. Somehow, money made it into their pockets without the use of hands.

I stood shorter than most of the crowd and tried to follow the flow of the spectacle. A cup suddenly pressed itself into my hand and the tea spilled over the top. Flinching from the burn I dropped some more. Greesbhaiji glared and scolded the man who had served me. Couldn't he see that I didn't know how to handle a hot cup? Why had he shoved the glass into my hand? Here, give the boy a saucer— and he showed me how to pour a portion from my glass onto the tiny plate, allowing it to cool and making it ready to sip. I remembered my father telling me that his grandfather always drank coffee in the same manner.

Greesbhaiji never looked at me when we walked in the street or drank chai on the corner. He always stared directly in front, as if surveying his territory. He would often mention his Kshatriya birth. He was a descendant of the caste of nobles and warriors, and his measured gaze never wavered in the company of others. Even when he spoke to me, which was rare, he did not look at me.

"Now you may go," he would say as the final sip rose to his parting lips. Before drinking he spoke, the cup already against his teeth. "I have some appointments I must keep with some elderly, some cancer patients, as you know, and then I have some students to tutor." Then he would drink, slow to the dregs, and return the cup. "So my Western friend, I must go. And you have learned something today, so I will see you tomorrow at ten o'clock sharp." With a smile he would pat my shoulder, then lean on it to turn himself in the direction in which he needed to walk. Thus I was sent off almost every afternoon.

One day during the nap period after lunch I was washing clothes in my room. My apartment was rather luxurious compared to my expectations. I enjoyed a private bathroom. Two buckets, meant for showering and flushing the toilet, served well for laundry also. During the first days when I was not even allowed to prepare my own plate at dinner, repeatedly plunging my hand into soapy water and wringing out my shirts offered a release. Working felt good. Through my grill window I could see the neighboring women a floor below me doing the same. My pants stuck to themselves with heavy flapping in the draft of the room. I felt glad to see that the water running down the seam and across the floor was clear. They had finally been liberated from a month's worth of well embedded dust.

Some bumping and low voices outside the door caught my wandering attention. I kept working but listened intently. They did not remain long. The conversation was broken from the beginning and it soon ended. A door closed and flip-flops flapped down the porch walk. But in the empty room another pair of feet scuttled lightly.

I lay on my bed for the rest of the hour with the shutters cracked just above my head. A taut beam of noon light sliced the upper quarter of the air and jabbed at the spare bookshelf across the room. I listened to the shuffling feet and then to the silence. My curiosity waned, and I dozed.

When I woke the usual stir in the courtyard made hearing movement next door impossible. Monks can be rowdy too, and some days seemed to inspire those of Khijada Mandir with the desire to take piggyback rides. We are all fools for the Lord, surely.

Greesbhaiji would be waiting. I hurriedly splashed my face and scampered down the stairs to avoid irritating him with my chronic tardiness. When I stepped into the shaded room I found him sitting near the door, opposite his usual perch, and he stood to meet me. Basantaji and another man with a quaint yellow cap sat in the far corner and made as if to rise.

"Your teacher has come," said Greesbhaiji with a great deal of dignity. He swept wide his arm toward the other two men and nodded in their direction. He meant for me to pass him by. The little monk beside Basantaji stepped nimbly forward. His eagerness evoked a light laugh in me. He bowed and smiled as broadly as a kindergarten teacher. "You are Mr. Scott Neely," he proclaimed, as if teaching me to be proud of my silly name. "And I am Vishwanatji. I am the one you communicated with before."

"Vishwanatji means 'Father of the World'," pronounced Greesbhai behind me. "So you should respect the wisdom of your teacher."

"There will be no problem with respect, we can see that well," said my teacher easily.

"No, but you read in the papers about these Western students and the things they do...," Greesbhaiji protested.

Vishwanatji's eyes did not leave me. "Yes, but there will be no problem." He spoke the words with such absence, he seemed to say that the conversation had no real significance. He appeared delighted with everything.

"I did not expect for you to come so soon, so I came when I heard you were here. I was with my old teacher in Mumbai and he encouraged me to come to you. Now, you have everything you need? No problem with food or water? No sickness?"

Greesbhaiji attested to my hosts' care. "He has been fine during these days."

"Good then. I will go now, to the temple, because I have been gone for some time, and I want to say hello." I understood that he meant to greet God and not his priestly colleagues. "So you will excuse me. My room is just beside yours, on the right. Come to see me after dinner, all right?"

"OK," I responded.

After brushing my teeth and washing up from dinner, I knocked on Vishwanatji's door. Beckoned to enter, I stepped inside the apartment. His room matched mine as a reflected image, everything identical and opposite in position, spare and neat. He sat with his legs folded on one bed, a little hunched in the back and supported in the front by his small paunch. On the other bed Basantaji sat with his legs crossed in formal Western fashion. His arm lay out across the knee, parallel to his extended leg, and he stopped speaking when I came across the threshold. A younger monk with a scraggly mustache and innocent eyes sat on the bed's far edge and listened without speaking.

"Come in, come in," Vishwanatji said excitedly. He might have been my grandfather. Basantaji made a place for me on the bed and I sat with the best posture I could muster. India never let me forget how inflexible my legs were and how weak my back was, especially during the times when all there was to do was wait.

"We have just been talking about your visit," he began. "I am very glad you are here. You did not have any problems?"

"No, everyone has been very kind," I responded politely.

"Yes, and your trip? The flight was good? Good. Your stay in Bihar did not have any difficulties? Good —you will see, or maybe you have already seen, that for Indians who do not live in Bihar, thinking of going there takes a lot of courage."

"Yes, I've heard that." I smiled and bowed my head to feign humility. "But I didn't know so much about Bihar before I went. I'm not sure ignorance qualifies as courage."

"Yes...," The word slipped through his teeth slowly. Then Vishwanatji regained his thought and said, "But it seems there is some misunderstanding of what you are going to do here."

"Yes," I looked up. "I hadn't realized I'd have my own teacher."

He knew my smile meant the politeness and the interest it expressed, and more as well. "And you thought you would be working."

I reined in the desire to explain everything at once and spoke slowly. "It is the point of my project. It's the way I carry out the study. I don't want to be in the way, but I want to work so that I can learn what you do here and why. I know I'm not so skilled, but anything is fine—I'll clean toilets, or sinks, or file papers, none of that matters. Just to be close to the work that is done here, that's what I'm after. So I can understand why you do it. But when I said this to the Maharajshri, he thought I would do better to study.

And he said there is no need for me to work here. So I'm not sure I really understand."

He spoke deliberately to try to make me see. "When your fax came, you see, no one understood it. So Maharaji sent for me because I speak and write English. It's actually my first language, really—grew up in an English language school in Mumbai, what you call Bombay. Yes. So I explained what you were after, and he agreed that you could come, although he didn't really understand what you were seeking. So I accepted to be your guide as per the Maharaji's conditions."

I looked at him a little askance. "So when I spoke to him a few days ago, he didn't really know that I thought I might be working here?"

"You met with Maharaji?" he asked.

"Yes, the afternoon I arrived he met with me. He had sent the faxes, and it's his name I had been given by my contact Mrs. Gandhi, so I thought I should speak to him."

He looked with glee at me and removed his glasses to rub his eyes. Dark circles looked painted under them. He continued smiling even with his lids shut. "To be honest, he did not exactly send you the faxes. I was given your first one, and after talking to Maharaji I wrote back. It seemed better to sign his name since he is the Maharajshri of this temple, but I wrote the letters. Which is why he still doesn't understand well why you are here. But don't worry," he leaned forward like an adolescent, "it won't be a bother. I'll explain it to him."

Basantaji shifted his legs, and we realized that we had forgotten the world around us. Grinning apologetically Vishwanatji turned to speaking Hindi and a slower English. For the rest of the night he explained some of the basic ideas in Hinduism and the historical particularities of Krishna Pranami thought.

That same joyfulness and independence of mind characterized the way Vishwanatji approached everything. A monk in his early twenties named Ram Daas, a favorite of the entire temple, ran to Vishwanatji every time he saw him. Ram Daas was mute and deaf and constantly excited about the simplest elements of life—birds passing overhead, wind rustling the monks' skirts. With his humor, handing him a cup of chai equaled him by telling a bawdy joke.

His innocence delighted Vishwanatji. When he saw Ram Daas running to meet him, Vishwanatji would alternately run even faster towards his would-be aggressor or hide behind the most solemn of the other monks, inevitably involving the stoic in the frolicking. He would occasionally tweak Daas's ear just to conjure his big toothed grin.

But his feistiness could turn bitter too. During my month's stay elder monks would slip into conversation comments about the possibility of my conversion. It was hard to determine if their insinuations simply poked fun at a hot political question of the time. Many non-Hindu groups and especially Christians in Gujarat had become the object of hate crimes by a militant Hindu organization. Although not at all a new problem in India, it had grown noticeably aggravated over the past Christmas season. The responsible militant group justified their terrorism as a response to Christianity's history of coercive conversion practices.

Vishwanatji took extreme exception to any teasing about my religious conviction, and more than once he raised his voice to protest a remark. We would meet nightly in his room for hours of religious dialogue and meditation. But his energy could never stay focused on just the subject at hand, and he would always gather in armfuls of examples from temple life to illustrate his points. One night after calling for me to come in he sat a long time in silence before opening his mouth. At last he opened his eyes and stared at me, discouraged.

"Do you know," he said slowly, "today one of those out there asked me if I had brainwashed you?" His tone was pinched in exasperation. I smiled, not without worry.

"Yes, brainwashed. I yelled at him for such stupidity. I don't understand why this keeps coming up, as if everybody had it in his head that you have to leave here a convert. Go back to the West and teach our religion, man! That's what they're thinking."

I tried to reassure him. "It'll be all right. It's not like it's going to happen, and the month will be up before you know it." But I also didn't understand, and I could comprehend his dismay. The entire point of my coming had been missed by the ashram, and my primary host could not seem to communicate to them the purpose of my visit.

His lamentation continued and he bowed his head. "Then I was asked to see Maharaji…"

"How was that?" I asked.

"He also wanted to know if you were becoming convinced of our ideas. He asked how the teaching was going and I responded, 'Very well,' that you were bright and eager to know the truth, and then he asked me if you were ready to accept the truth. Which means this Krishna Pranami religion! And I couldn't stop myself, I shouted back that no one was trying to convert you and certainly not me, and that you would be the one to make all of the decisions about what you believed!"

"What happened then?" I ventured after a moment.

"He laughed and told me to watch my blood pressure...," he mumbled. His hurt showed. "Do you see this?" he asked while motioning to his bottom front teeth. They had eroded to little more than nubs barely raised above the gum line. "You'd think I just had bad teeth from the prasad, but it's from grinding them together. All my life. I was always known for my temper. Once, when I was an engineer in Mumbai and a manager tried to provoke a worker on strike, I turned and gave him a good one. Right in the jaw. And you can see my height—he must have been six inches taller than I, at least, but he wasn't after that. You see I'm short but pretty strong." The story unraveled into the night to cheer us.

In the end, the confusion over my reason for visiting the temple served as my ticket into the medical clinic. Vishwanatji decided that in order to help people understand more fully my visit I needed to be made increasingly visible and focused on my stated task. He and I had been making daily trips outside of the ashram to visit local non-government and social service organizations. A Jain woman in the city had adopted the service side of my education, leaving the contemplative theology to Vishwanatji. We would meet her at her house and pay visits to social and

political leaders, discussing with them the relationship between religion and service, dharma and seva.
But even if told, the others at Khijada Mandir could
not know what we were doing.

My willingness to participate in the temple rituals
began to seem ill advised to Vishwanatji, too. One
morning he said to me over milk, "Maybe go in a little
late after breakfast. And then don't go at all for the
rest of the day. We'll see from day to day what is best."

His game plan consisted of isolation and visible
purpose—don't give them what they want and do
what you need to do. The degree to which he meant
to abide by the strategy came to seem like a reaction
against a conspiracy theory, but I followed it closely.
He dedicated himself to helping his guest achieve
some semblance of his original purpose, and I drew
on his determination. One night he ended our discussion by calling to me at the door as I left. "Tomorrow
morning, let's visit the clinic together."

Though minor, the tone of the act would not go
unnoticed. Our independence was defiant if indirect.
Vishwanatji confided in me his fear that as a convert
himself and a newcomer to the temple, he might be
asked to leave if the situation degenerated to a
squabble. Having become a renouncer of the world
at the time of his retirement and his wife's death, his
position in the ashram was far more tenuous than
that of the lifelong ascetics, the very people with
whom he had crossed words.

But as we crossed the plaza the next morning we
met a tone of cheer. Old monks lined up for diabetes
shots patted me on the back and gripped my neck
with rough tenderness. Inside the small rooms the

monks serving as pharmacists and nurses seemed only surprised. Far from being an act of revolution, my presence simply delighted them. Some had thought I slept past this hour because Vishwanatji and I left so early every morning.

No work needed to be done and so we asked permission of the doctor if we might stand in a corner and observe. He assented austerely but soon loosened after growing accustomed to my gaze. A partial wall divided the pharmacy and the examination room. I stood between the two to watch the movement of patients through their stations. As the morning passed I scribbled like a stenographer in my notebook, not watching the page in order to keep my mind on the people. If I could not work in the clinic I would absorb it through my pencil. I followed the stream of people and consciousness.

At 9:00 the work had not yet begun. A line of women wound outside the grating into the street. One watched trucks and bicycles shake by and her breath rolled out of itself in the still warming air. The women chattered and rubbed their lips and their teeth stained by the same starchy diet over the past forty years.

The dispensary looked more like a kitchen than a pharmacy. On a low table I saw one monk, Luxma, placing needles in a sterilization box that looked something like a toaster.

The hunched teacher of the sect's religious texts waddled in on his cane. Always the same sliver of yellow tilak, a line of paint indicating that one has been to prayer, like the smudged crosses of Ash Wednesday, streaked his forehead. He rolled up his sweater sleeve for a shot of insulin. All of the middle-aged and elderly monks suffered from diabetes, the result of a rice-based diet and a handful of sugared prasad with every visit to the temple. He could not pull the sweater high enough and scowled, poking his shoulder through the unbuttoned neck of his polyester shirt. The doctor casually slipped the cold needle into his flat and hairy lower shoulder, slowly pressed in the liquid, and pulled the syringe out. The old man jiggled his muscles to loosen them up, wrapped himself in his brown wool blanket and went into the morning.

I was wrong for the times in India when I re-proached people for their casualness and apparent lethargy. The drowsy eyed doctor with a sandy voice and distant attitude scrawled prescriptions on torn slips of paper for an hour every morning and then went to the hospital for a day's work. He served the people in his manner, with kindness they understood as comfort.

On his forehead too a fleck of orange marked that he had been to the temple. He knew his work and did it. He labored with bodies. Each sheet in his folder read a name and the history of a personal medical geography that he had traveled.

A pudgy and creaking old woman hobbled into the examination room and rolled back into a folding chair. Her tilak smeared huge, vermilion, the full width of her nose bridge, and ran from her stocking cap to the narrowing curve between her clean eye-brows. She chewed her gums and rocked, and I wondered how she smelled. Her feet swaggled above the floor, and sometimes she would groan out high-pitched words, like water bubbling out of a long settled outcropping, gurgling.

An elegant man entered with a calm face. It was also stricken and closed, maybe from the sunken eyes and high bridging above them. He sat down and his brown coat puckered awkwardly. I glanced down to jot notes on him and he had gone before I looked back up.

The old woman was still sitting in the folding chair. She wore no shoes. Her feet soles were thickly callused and the tops of her feet cracked with dry white lines beneath the skin's surface, like ice in the late fall.

In the neighboring room Luxma received prescriptions and filled reused bottles of medicine. Silver trays reflecting hundreds of colored pills covered the two counters. Patients listened attentively to his directions and remembered. Nothing was written down.

A well-groomed boy of 14 or 15 came in and sat in the patients' chair. Compared to her son's unassuming grace, his buck-toothed mother, clothed in red under a beige sweater, evoked in me a feeling of pity.

The doctor looked the son over and the boy and mother exited. An old woman stepped in and did not stop talking until the doctor finished and sent her out. In the chatter I caught her name, Pusanabhen. The doctor checked her pulse with brief, certain movements.

A little girl entered with her mother. When asked to stick out her tongue so that the doctor could inspect her throat, she could not open her mouth wide enough for her fear. When her mother removed the girl's pale blue pullover for the stethoscope she cried as if she wanted to retreat but found herself immobile. Her mother's long sheer black throw made her beautiful, forbidding. She stood thin with large diamond earrings.

A man kicked his left heel into the chair and showed large blistering around the outer ankle, white and dry like burnt wood. I imagined a purple smudging of dust around it, similar to what I had seen on Greesbhaiji's infected foot each day. His skin was darkly tarnished and his hair white, prickly, smudged in brown.

The man in the brown jacket returned and leaned against the far partition behind which the waiting room was positioned. He stood within himself, closed to the surrounding commotion. In his white pajama pants and pinstriped shirt under the jacket, he was clean. I could see his bones slide out like webbing with his veins under blue rubber flip-flops. His ears looped large and clean.

Then a man barged into the examination room, unwashed and blundering. He writhed everywhere, found the bed against the wall and sprawled across it.

The patient receiving attention scowled, and the doctor excused himself. He came to the man and attended to him calmly, exactly, his keen eye and ear cutting straight down to the appendix. He scribbled a note and called an attendant to accompany the man to the hospital.

I watched Luxma clean used syringes in between prescriptions and then prepare them for reuse. He would slip the upturned needle into the inverted cap of a bottle of clear pink liquid and slowly draw back the plunger. When he filled the needles he brought them to be used immediately, forming a row of hypodermics and little balls of moist cotton laid out beside the doctor's forearm.

From time to time Luxma would wash his hands, and red soap bled into the basin.

Outside across the road a gang of four young kids strutted around in suits, one with sunglasses on as the leader.

A girl sat, her black hair pulled slick and tightly back, her frame composed.

Another waited dully, with a tiny diamond in her nose's fine curve.

At almost 10:00 the hall was still jammed with people. Without question they excelled at waiting.

When it came time for me to move on to another city I would reimburse my hosts for the generosity they had shown me during my stay. Keeping an exact tab of expenses was not always easy and some people —Basantaji, for example—deliberately attempted to sneak costs past me so that I could not repay them. Occasionally we achieved a degree of playful deceit that brought the question to the point at which it should have stayed all along—friends finding the joy in assisting one another in their appointed tasks.

At the end of February I found myself low on cash. In Chiang Mai and Bihar I had left reimbursements as gifts in U.S. dollars, the value being greater and more stable than the local currency. Having neither access to nor need of an ATM since coming to India, and not knowing what might be required of my pocketbook before making the last plane out of New Delhi, I felt skittish about using my last actual dollar bills to pay the ashram. I decided to exchange some traveler's checks in order to make the "donation". But when I arrived at the Saurastra State Bank and showed my checks, the clerk frowned.

"Sorry, we don't exchange traveler's checks here. Try the State Bank of India, Jhoti Gate."

So off I went, but there the same grimace met me. "Try the Corporation Bank, down the alley and across the main intersection."

But there the foreign exchange clerk would not even look at me after seeing my American Express checks. "We don't take those here," he scowled and retreated back into his smoky office.

I went to plead my case before my hosts at the temple. "You shouldn't have gone alone," Greesbhaiji concluded with his gruff wisdom, referring to the world-renowned nod-nod-wink-wink connection and name dropping system that is a way of life in India. "I know people in the Baroda Bank and there are friends of this temple at Saurastra Bank. Tomorrow there'll be no problem."

The next day we set out, me stumbling between the long, certain strides of scholars (Greesbhaiji), sages (Vishwanatji), and saints (Basantaji). They dispelled doubt like Moses before the Red Sea. Elegant and luminous in their dhotis, they incarnated virtue, dignity, determination. Having my checks turned down now was an impossibility. They certified that my money was good.

We hit five banks that day in over four hours of walking and arguing. No luck. Finally, at a little corner branch of the State Bank of India, we got our explanation.

"Jamnagar is a port town," the clerk said to me. "Sometimes the sailors steal from the passengers. Recently some stole American Express Traveler's Cheques and made Xerox copies of them. One of the banks in Jamnagar cashed them unknowingly—but now American Express won't stand by their agreement and reimburse the bank. So we are all boycotting American Express business."

I thought their solidarity remarkable. The answer satisfied and actually impressed me. I did not really need the money anymore, having opted to care for the donation with the cash I had with me anyway. An explanation was all I had wanted. But my hosts were not sated in the least.

"He's our guest, he deserves—"

"A university student from America—"

"I know Kishorbhai your president and I'll tell you, sir—"

"What if we sign a document assuming responsibility?"

The question now was honor, not my own, but my hosts'. As their guest, every need of mine should be met. They would go to any extreme to make sure it was. I tried to assuage them. "Look, I really don't need the money. I've taken care of the donation. Let's just drop it."

Vishwanatji heard me and assented, but Greesbhaiji held firm. "What?" He seemed almost furious. "You're going to Mumbai, and I have been there. I know the kind of money you will need. So let's go." He could not hear that I would not even be leaving the airport in Bombay, and the force of his conviction persuaded Vishwanatji to stay quiet.

To Greesbhaiji, there was no going back. Spouting nonsense that acquiesced to denial only showed that, revered guest though I might be, I was also a naïve foreign youngster who could learn from the way maturity handled the situation. So I went along for the ride. But the fact that the origin of the situation— my need—had disappeared into the greater debacle of honor denied had begun to frustrate me.

After two more days and a dizzying ring of connections, notes, and banks entered and exited, I changed a token U.S. $40 in American Express Traveler's Cheques. Everyone beamed and slapped one another on the back, swapping stories of relatives in high positions, of old high school and underground Communist days. The team had won, with the exception of the clerk and me.

His stare meant to bring me down to my trouble-making knees. "I trust," he glowered, stiffly handing me the rupees, "that you won't need any more money than this…"

Hospitality was the virtue of my month in Jamnagar, hospitality that exceeded the constraints of wisdom and reason. Pride held sway over Khijada Mandir, a kind of irresponsible desire to do everything for the guest—cloth him, feed him, house him, get religion into him, bank for him—even at my expense.

A real goodness showed through our fallibilities and egotism. Self-love and love merged.

The Saints

After leaving Vishwanathji one night, as I sat late
composing in my notebook, a light knock came to
the door, so soft I waited to hear it again before
responding. I slipped across the apartment floor and
opened the door to the cool evening. Basantaji stood
there, and as I opened the way he stepped into the
room. One hand bore a silver cup, the other held
something that crinkled in its cellophane wrapper.

"Come in, please," I said, though he was already
past me in the room. As the temple manager I suppose he had the right to act so boldly, but he needed
no excuse. The certainty and dignity with which he
carried himself rendered any welcoming formality on
my part superfluous.

He placed the cup on the bookshelf and leaned
towards one of the candles burning nearby as he
turned his attention to the contents of his other hand.
The wrapper came off and he placed it in his shirt
pocket. Then he took what looked like a green disk
in one hand and tried numerous times to push something into it. This done, he perched the weird model
on the bookshelf, pulled a lighter out of his pocket,
and held the flame lightly against the disk's edge. The
flame flared for a moment and then he pocketed the
lighter. A blunt little ember glowed against the disk.

Still silent, he reached to the opposite wall and
turned the fan on to its lowest setting.

"For the mosquitoes," he said, smiled, and bowed
curtly before he walked out of the door. He pulled it
closed behind him before I could reach it, and my
thanks never passed the threshold. The soft smell of
incense wafted past my nose, and in the candlelight

I saw thin wisps of smoke pulled into the fan's lazy rotation, then pushed out on its wind into the room's corners.

I walked over to the cup and lifted it. A thin film had formed on the milk's warm surface, and I drank.

What religion need be studied, what theology learned, when such a basic act of care forms all of the friendship and happiness we desire? I was studying infant saints impatient for maturity, and Basantaji stood amongst us, silently certain of the purpose of heaven.

Jerusalem, Israel, Palestine
7 March 1999 – 5 April 1999

A city blooms from the hills,
Grown by its own mountains.

As if an earthquake could build walls,
Anger knots its stones together.

By 5:30 I was up and leaning over a dirty basin
rinsing sleep from my eyes. Still clear from the night,
the sky was clean and the cold chafed my cheeks.
Looking east I could see the Judean Desert fall where
the Jordan Valley lay concealed and then rise again
into the Jordanian Mountains. With hands still purple
and thick from the water, I pushed my sweatshirt
sleeves back down, arranged my blue stocking cap
over wet hair, and picked up the shovel propped in
the bathroom corner. In those March mornings before
Pesach and Easter, the mountains around Zion lay like
lions. Three hours before breakfast I would walk into
the gardens of the Diaspora Yeshiva Toras Israel and
begin uprooting the weeds that broke the even white
pavement between stones.

A yeshiva is a center for instruction and debate
in the Torah, the Hebrew Bible, for men who have

devoted themselves to the highest mitzphah, or 'good work', in Judaism—the study of God's law. Yeshivas are similar to other types of seminaries, a congregation of students and families forming a community of religious practice and learning. Diaspora Yeshiva Toras Israel, located on the southern slope of Mount Zion just outside of Jerusalem's Old City walls, was established after the 1948 war that claimed Palestine as the geographic home of the new state of Israel. The founder of the yeshiva, Rosh-Yeshiva Goldstein, fought to take the ground on which his community is now located. As one walks through the gates into Old Jerusalem's Jewish Quarter, holes left by shelling pock the high white wall.

I had not come to Israel for an extended stay in Jerusalem. My plan involved only a short visit to the capital after a longer month of work and travel in northwestern Haifa, bordering the Mediterranean. Before leaving the United States to begin my trip I had communicated extensively with SHATIL, an umbrella service organization that routes foreign volunteers interested in working in Israel to agencies and non-governmental organizations that fit their interests. I'd been given some information on a student peace coalition of Arab and Jewish Israelis. They called themselves Re'ut Sadaka, the words for friendship in both Hebrew and Arabic. Their emphasis on moving towards co-existence as well as their location in a less politicized area of Israel piqued my interest. Contact had just been established with them when I disappeared into two months of tele- phone and e-mail silence in India, and only after resurfacing in Tel Aviv did I have the opportunity to again communicate with the group. But no response to my last e-mail awaited me when I was able to get back on-line, and repeated attempts at contacting them were answered with silence. For three days I frequented Tel Aviv's cyber cafes waiting to hear how to find the group's offices and whether or not I would be welcome in Haifa. I enjoyed the days of lounging by the warming sea and nights on jetties with bedraggled widowers and fishermen, watching their broken hands mending lines and casting heavy sinkers and live bait into the black surf. News of bombings on the Syrian border had worried me as I boarded the flight from Zurich, but Tel Aviv seemed unruffled by the threat of open conflict. The buzzing media inhabited an atmosphere above us, irrelevant to the business of flipping coins from my pocket for a couple of falafels. But restlessness nagged at me and I returned constantly to the keyboards and black tea of the coffee houses downtown. After half a week passed without word, I decided to take a bus north to try my luck without further invitation.

Another half-week of circling through Haifa taught me the city well. I wandered through the industrial quarter and its adjoining blue-collar and Russian immigrant neighborhoods, up through the main streets below Mount Carmel and then into the wealthier suburbs, looking first for the evasive Tourist Office, then beyond the city to the mountaintop Haifa University, and finally into the Arab neighborhoods in search of the office of Re'ut Sadaka. Conversations with security guards at Haifa University revealed that the group was not affiliated with the school, although many students were associated with the organization.

Sunday afternoon after my first quiet Shabbat in
Israel, I meandered through graded streets in the
Arab quarter looking for the organization's office.
Numbers skipped by tens and reversed back down
toward zero, jumping whole buildings and hiding
in alleys. I rounded the corner of a walled basketball
court, dragging my finger along the chain-link fence.
Kids in beaten jeans taunted each other and skidded
across the concrete, a goalie diving for the soccer ball,
a first-grader sliding to tackle his overweight brother.

Below the game I found the right street but back-
tracked three times without finding the building,
the numbers playing games with me again. I walked
across the street and motioned to a group of men
chatting in the open door of a mechanic's shop. The
one wiping oil from his hands smiled, pardoned
himself from the gathering, and stepped into the
street.

"Ish?" he said, asking me what was needed.

"Re'ut Sadaka? Re'ut Sadaka?" I pronounced slowly,
questioning in a word. He pointed opposite us to a
little placard on the second story façade. Two ginger-
bread figures, one blue, one black, held hands above
Hebrew and Arabic script.

"Yes, yes," he nodded as I looked over my shoulder
to him, moving toward a narrow door under the sign.
The display window beside it was opaque with dust.
A fissure ran through a pane in the door window. The
men in the mechanic shop had stopped talking and
watched me, chuckling a little. One waved his hand
over his head with the motion of a quarterback, and
I stepped into the dark hall.

At the landing, the door to the second floor office

stood ajar. I knocked, pushing it open slightly to glimpse in. Through another door computers hummed unattended, and two men huddled over one. They argued over the bleeping pot shots of a video game and the occasional explosion of their targets. I knocked louder. A thinly bearded, slight man turned to look at the door, bent back over his friend for a moment and checked his watch. Then he came to the entrance and opened the door wide, standing behind it and holding his body over the doorknob.

"Alo?" He scanned me like a nervous squirrel.

"Hello—I...I'm sorry, I don't speak Hebrew or Arabic." I was less embarrassed than I might have been since I'd communicated, if briefly, with an office worker in good North American English via e-mail. Despite the quavering insecurity in my voice, I held my gaze to his face. His eyes flitted restlessly.

"But you do speak English," he stated flatly, barely betraying his thoughts. High along his left cheek and almost to his eye, the muscles pulled a little and then relaxed. "Und Deutsch?"

"Nein, mais un peu de français—," I offered.

"For me English is better," he ventured hesitantly. Then regaining his confidence he asked, "How may I help you?"

I offered my hand and introduced myself. "I wrote some months ago about volunteering here. I wrote and Sarah answered saying it would be all right to come and see what you do."

He swept his arm languidly in front of the door and stepped away from the threshold. "Come in, please. Here, sit here." I walked to a long linoleum-topped table and set my bag on its top. He slipped

behind me and fumbled with a fan's electrical wire
wrapped around chair legs. He passed to the window
and glanced out, then eased into a rolling chair and
wheeled it to the table's end like a street kid playing
in a CEO's empty office. I feigned a smile and waited
for him to make the first move. "Wait just a moment,"
he said, remembering something, and went back to
the computer game room. A phone ring brought him
quickly back to the desk. "Alo, yeah...Sorry, just a
moment, please, sorry," he said to me again. I waved
off his excuse and glanced over the office. Posters in
German and French with multicultural kids dancing
over the world. A map of Israel in yellow and
splotches of pink, marked in Arabic and blocky
Hebrew script. A reproduced print of a dove, Picasso-
esque. Roughly organized stacks of paper weighted
by a baseball, a glass, stones, the paper edges flutter-
ing as the fan pivoted. The darkening street through
the window, and his fingers wiggling in the curling
phone cord.

"I am sorry," he repeated, hanging up slowly. "You
have spoken with Sarah before?"

I explained the process of seeking a volunteer
group in Israel, of being passed from Israeli acquaintances of professors to a couple of NGOs and SHATIL,
and finally to a few e-mails exchanged with Sarah on
the part of Re'ut Sadaka.

"I did not read your messages, I do not take care of
the e-mails and message arrangements and so forth."
He paused as if catching himself. "I'm sorry again. I'm
Amith, I work here also coordinating the group meetings and living in the community." His apologies were
always somehow dulled, through distance created by

his distrust of his English ability or through a natural wariness that moved under our conversation. He reached out his hand and I took it, shaking once and discreetly wiping my hand on my jean's leg under the table as he continued talking. "I work here, we work here, I do, along with," and I missed the name for my lack of familiarity with Semitic languages, "there in the back. Here we work full-time, all day, and then there are some half-time workers who maybe help with communications or meetings, and then also volunteers. The volunteers work hard but are not paid. We all live here in Haifa now but we come from all over this country, Israel, Palestine.

"But the problem is that Sarah is not here now and I do not know when she is coming back. Hey," and he called the man in the next room by name, switching to Arabic, "do you know when Sarah is coming back, if she's coming today again or no?" He called back that she wasn't.

"Well, maybe I should come tomorrow sometime to meet with her," I suggested, feeling for my place in the conversation and his stance on my being there.

"No, that's all right. I mean you don't have to go yet. Where are you from, from the States or Canada?"

"The U.S., yes."

"And what would you like, to work here? But why work here at Re'ut Sadaka?" His question had none of the self-conscious humility with which I'd become so familiar with Sister Jessi. The interest and skepticism in his tone made me feel almost as if I was applying for a permanent position. I summarized as best I could the idea of my scholarship and the project I'd undertaken. The possibility of working with a group organizing for peace rather than with an individual as I'd done in the preceding months interested me, especially if it was a group of people my own age. So I did want to volunteer and by volunteering to learn about the problems of racism and peace in Israel. Amith nodded and bounced a pencil from eraser to point to eraser as I spoke. I finished and searched his face again for some idea of how all this stood with him. I was apparently a new fish in his experience. He certainly hadn't expected a volunteer to arrive that evening.

"You see," he resumed after a short silence, "I cannot suggest that you stay here to work. I am sorry Sarah is not here because you obviously wrote with her and she knew you were coming sometime. Maybe she didn't know it would be today, but sometime."

I checked a smirk from surfacing. It was a little hard to believe that I'd been searching for Re'ut Sadaka for over a week, on foot and on-line, and that once found I was going to be sent right back out into the Sunday dusk of a new week. Amith continued with his apology and explanation. "But I don't think there is really something for you to do here anyway. Maybe you could help with the newsletter or something. But you don't speak Arabic or Hebrew, and to speak both is best if you want to join in our discussion groups. But you must have one, the leaders could not take all the time to explain what everyone was saying to you while they tried to direct a meeting. So...so."

"It seems that I should probably keep looking for something else. If I can't help here, or anywhere, then I don't want to interfere. I don't want to be in the way."

He looked up to be sure we understood each other. "It's not that you couldn't stay, but what would you do? What would you understand?" He picked up his pencil again.

"Well," I exhaled, edging the conversation to a close.

"But do you have some time now? Of course, you had come here for today, you have nowhere to go now. Because if you have some time, I can talk to you about what we do here."

I took the offer. He was willing to talk about his work, and I had come to help him. At least I'd find out what he did before I walked out the door. And, ever the mildly opportunistic optimist, I entertained the possibility that in the course of our talk he might show me around, something might develop, I might find myself suited with a job, no matter how menial, by the meeting's end.

"The most important work we do here," he began, "is our youth meetings. We have groups of Arab and Jewish Israelis, like our age, meeting once or twice a week to talk."

"What of?"

"About trying to live!" he enunciated and cast a mild glance of ridicule my way. Throughout that year of conversations I always appealed to naiveté rather than assume understanding of any given topic. Appearing innocent or outrightly stupid might have earned me vague disdain on occasion, but a fuller explication was almost always gained. Amith took the famous Jewish—Arab Israeli conflict and moved into a deeper explanation of it.

"It's not just about fighting and wars, but that is

also a part. You have read about the Syrian problem going on now? But the papers don't say much about the jeep that general was in, the one killed, that it was probably in a zone they knew they should not cross. People antagonize the situation to cause problems here, but we do not hear about it being openly discussed. Probably you do not hear about it in the papers back in the United States. When I was in Germany, for a conference about youth organizations for peace," he brushed aside bragging about the chance to travel by sweeping his hand lazily in the air, "the newspapers were the same as here when they talked about Israel. Always the incomplete truth, so we have to fill in the story and guess.

"But it's not just about wars. The wars helped cause all this—you know about Zionism? Okay—but we are not always shooting at each other. It's inside that we are angry and fighting, and see," he set the pencil down sharply and leaned over the desk towards me, "Israel is supposed to be a democracy. The citizens of a democracy should all have the same rights and be treated the same. But in Israel," he turned away again, spinning a quarter turn to look out the window, then swiveling his chair back towards me, "it is not the same. It is more like fascism." I leaned forward in my chair and wondered if he really meant what he was saying. He clearly did. I'd never heard a statement like that before, though I conceded as questionable the undemocratic practice of immediately naturalizing all Jews upon arrival in the Ben Gurion International Airport in Tel Aviv while eyeing everyone else with discomforting scrutiny. But I had chalked that up to the demands of security. "It is like you had in the United States when the Africans could not have their civil rights. Arabs here are hated by Jews and because we built the system, the system hates Arabs too."

"How do you hate them?"

Amith pulled back sharply and then relaxed into the high chair back. "I, I do not hate them." He pointed to himself. "But Jews hate Arabs. And Arabs hate Jews. That is why we have our youth group meetings. We will get together and say to the Arabs, 'Think of every stereotype you have of Jews. Think of everything your parents have said to you and that you see in the movies.' And the same for Jews, thinking about Arabs. And then we say to both groups, 'Now think about the stereotypes about Arabs if you are an Arab. And act it out for us.' So we have like a show, Arabs complaining how stupid and lazy Arabs are— and you can hear everyday, every time in the street people yelling and complaining that some Jew said that he was lazy or stupid—and Jews saying how racist they are, and how they have no morals if they are secular and are wrong and hateful if they are religious. So they see each other the way they hate each other. And sometimes the first year of meetings will end every week in people yelling at each other. But if they stay together to really work on this, after sometime they can start to really talk. And then the directors from Re'ut Sadaka do not have to spend all of their time shouting louder than everyone else to keep it quiet." He snickered at his joke and then sobered. "So those youth groups are the most important, because it's how we try to learn to see another person as really human without just hating him because he is a Jew or Arab."

"And do you think it is working?"

"Yes, it is working. I am here to say it is working. All of the people who direct a youth group have been in the program. I went into one when I was in what you call 'high school'. And now it is the work I do. But we cannot be the only people trying to help."

"But you're not the only people trying to help, are you? SHATIL is finding foreign volunteers for hundreds of organizations."

Amith jerked upright in his chair. For a moment he studied my waiting face. Then he started talking, and the three hours of conversation that ensued were dedicated to peeling back the onion skin layers of my ignorance.

He began by talking about Zionism and its wide acceptance in Israeli thought. SHATIL, he made clear on no uncertain terms, was a Zionist organ despite whatever humanitarian intentions might motivate its employees. He explained Zionism as being completely ingrained in mainstream politics and social structures, so pervasive an idea that almost no one questioned whether it was in practice truly viable or just. He talked about the peripheral nature of an organization like Re'ut Sadaka. The work of co-existence and civil equality between Jewish and Arabic Israelis is uncommon in Israel. The resentment of the Youth Congress of Haifa University was provoked when foreign organizations began inviting Re'ut Sadaka to participate in international symposia to the exception of more Zionist groups. "It is true that we do not represent majority Jewish Israeli thought," he chuckled. "But that says something important too."

The conversation jumped from subject to subject. He didn't want to leave anything out. My time with him was short, regardless of how long we might talk that evening, and he evangelized me without pause that I might go warily to the wolves in the street. It was unlikely that I'd hear the same perspective during my coming month in Israel. Jewish Israelis would not share it or support discussion of it, and Arab Israelis would not be in a linguistic or social situation to speak of it. So he talked, growing more animated as time passed. With the devotion of a monk tapping beads, he recited a litany of falsehoods and injustices suffered by Palestinians and the cause of a just democracy at the hands of practices he described as colonial, racist, and fascist. He testified to the destruction of Palestinian homes throughout contemporary Israel during the 1948 War of Independence, and the streetlights hummed on. From the creation of a virtual Palestinian refugee state he traced continuing injustices up to the present-day policy of destroying Arab Israeli homes in the name of "street expansion" and "infrastructure renewal". Down in the street, kids were called home and took their last shots on goal. Headlights began to flash across the wall opposite me. He continued, unrelenting, insatiable in his desire to rectify the wrongs still being perpetrated by feeding me everything he could cram into one sitting. The injustices of the Israeli state passed easily to condemnation of Western nations, and especially of the United States, for their support of the "fascist" government. He joked about CIA cooperation with the Mossad, Israel's crack intelligence bureau, and the agents that try to infiltrate Re'ut Sadaka's meetings.

"They try to mess up your work?"

"Of course, like they do with anything they don't agree with. We are dangerous, we want things different." He smiled. He clearly enjoyed the idea, but not so much as to cloud the sincerity of his real desire for justice. "But we can always tell who they are. We know of someone now in our group and we just let them know that they can leave anytime. We have nothing to hide anyway. Maybe they will understand what we are saying and change too. And when we go out of the country, you can always tell who is following us. He takes all the same planes as you do. So I will walk up to the guy and start speaking in Hebrew, asking what he thinks he's doing and if he really is so secretive. Then the secret is gone and he loses most of his strength to do much hurting."

Late in the conversation a woman had walked into the office. She looked twice when she noticed me and then disappeared into the adjoining office for a time. Afterwards she came back out and sat at the far end of the table, listening to our discussion without commenting.

Suddenly Amith finished and begged my forgiveness. "I hadn't seen the time passing, I'm sorry," he stuttered, self-conscious again and stumbling over English for the first time in hours. "Ah, Sarah," he said as he noticed the woman seated across from us. He got up to introduce us, but she stood and cut him short.

"Oh, that's all right," she said cheerily. "I figured you must be Scott from, well, you're speaking English with him, Amith. Nice to meet you. I'm originally from Washington state myself." We shook hands.

"Look," I apologized, "I'd lost track of time too and I've got to get back to my hostel. Dinner'll be finished and things'll close up soon."

"Let me walk you out," she said. Amith had disappeared into the computer room and stepped out briefly to wish me well. He apologized again for the time and for the lack of work to be done. I thanked him. He'd made more than enough space for me.

In the cooling evening I could feel how excited the talk with Amith had made me. My body held its own warmth and my head was buzzing with ideas. He'd completely redefined the way I saw everything around me. Even if he was wrong about some things—and I couldn't know for certain whether or not he was—the possibilities he'd suggested imploded the image of Israel I'd formed for 22 years, a pseudo-religious and democratic vision of the righteous state.

"Listen, sorry there's nothing here for you," Sarah apologized. "I thought there would be. But I want to tell you something—I don't know what you did in there, but you must be the world's best listener. I've never heard Amith talk like that. How'd you get him to tell you all those things?"

"He just started talking."

"Well."

"Anyway, thanks for inviting me to come. It's been worth it despite whatever disappointment—"

"If you come again to Israel, let me know. I'll find something for you."

I turned from the first week and the possibility of working in Re'ut Sadaka. Perhaps it was best not to join them for however brief a time. A U.S. American student who pops in out of nowhere could only be underfoot and provoke unhelpful suspicion, certainly of myself if not of the group. But the search for the little Haifa peace and coexistence group had not been in vain. That night was one of those moments when I walked back home differently than the way I'd left it.

The next day I left for Jerusalem. I'd gathered a rough list of various NGOs that might accept a short-term volunteer, and most required my physical presence to further investigate the possibilities of work. I dozed on the bus and then opened my eyes to the growing hills.

One could not enter a more beautiful city. Coming from the northeast the bus rose into low mountains. The city began to gather around us, building itself out of scattered boulders and limestone outcroppings into residential neighborhoods, hospitals, universities, all constructed in golden white Jerusalem stone. Unlike any other city that I have ever seen, Jerusalem seemed to grow from the mountains upon which it is situated, rather than imposing itself on a landscape.

But the beauty was embittered by Haifa's lessons. The question of the justice of Israel's brief national history tempered my enthusiasm for the aesthetic achievement of the city. It seemed almost like a fortress against suspicion and rebuke, a construction too white and perfected for reproach. So I became increasingly dubious of Israel's appearance.

My search for volunteer work and saints unraveled as days passed. Security concerns forced almost every organization to require an extended application process before anyone could carry out their garbage, and I spent days hopping from office to office until gradually my resolve weakened. I spent more and more time wandering Jerusalem, enjoying the confusion of alleys inside the Old City's walls contrasted with clear ethnic divisions outside in the new streets. But the lack of direction and work frustrated me. One day I sat on a low wall and pulled out my notebook, jotting notes and trying to gain some sense of purpose. A worn mantra repeated itself exasperatedly in my head. 'God,' I thought, 'if there is something for me to do other than tramp around Israel during this month, could we please get on with it.'

"This is a good place to study," a voice above me remarked. Two little black shoes pointed at me from under my notebook.

"Is it?" I replied, looking up to see a shaggy bearded man studying me intently.

"Yes. Do you know where you are? The tomb of Holy King David is just a couple hundred yards from here, just through those doors." He gestured towards the alcove through which I'd just walked.

"Is it," I said as I looked back at him. Never before had I felt so jealous of the ability to grow facial hair prolifically. His bushy beard striated into a thousand tightly curled strands, beginning reddish-brown near his chin and dissipating into light gray towards his chest. His loose-fitting black jacket was dusty and crumpled.

"It is," he ruminated. Returning to me, he introduced himself as a rabbi and a school teacher originally from Kansas City but long-established in Jerusalem.

"I'm a student," I returned and then explained the basic idea of my trip. "And I'm unestablished anywhere for the moment."

"Well, this is a yeshiva," he continued amiably. "Are you Jewish?" he regressed for a moment, trying to get his bearings.

"No."

"Do you know what a yeshiva is?"

"No, sir."

The explanation became a walking tour of the facility. I had apparently seated myself in the middle of the campus. As we began to walk, an old man in exceedingly baggy black clothes and a thick sweater strode up to us. His beard outdid the rabbi's in length and mass. It looked as if he'd been pulling on the left side of it all morning.

"Hi," he said in a thick New York accent. His hands kneaded each other restlessly.

"Rebbe, this is—," the rabbi began. He chased my name for a moment and I rescued him.

"Hi," the man repeated. "What are you doing here?" There was no malice in his voice. His question was almost a joke. He just wanted to know where my feet were going. His thin frame quivered from an excess of energy, as if he had to fight to keep from breaking spontaneously into jumping jacks.

"Talking with the rabbi. In Jerusalem? Trying to find some volunteer work for the next couple of weeks," I answered.

"Are you Jewish?" he asked. I shook my head. "Do you want to be?"

At this I laughed. "We go slowly, no?!"

"Well, we need work done here before Pesach— you know Pesach, Passover? You could stay here to work and study in the evenings. It's a good place for it. Anyway, you decide." As quickly as he'd begun questioning us he scampered off in the direction from which he'd come.

"That's the Rosh-Yeshiva, the head of this yeshiva," the rabbi said. "Now that's something." We watched the old man scramble up the street and duck through a gate. "Shall we?" he asked, and we continued walking.

We walked past a schoolroom just when a rush of boys swarmed out, all in black or navy sweaters and wearing kipahs, small circular caps worn in reverence to God. We entered a quiet courtyard and the rabbi reached for the handle of a large wooden door that had sunken into its frame. "Keep that on," he advised me and motioned to my stocking cap.

He lugged the door open. Voices like the din of the tide pressed through the entranceway and moved around the walls inside. As we stepped in I found myself in a small series of stone rooms under an arched ceiling. Books stood half again my height on tables and filled shelves that met the ceiling's seam with the walls. Everywhere men were reading, talking, some even yelling at each other. One snoozed oblivious to three standing around him. They rocked like candle flames and read under their breath, holding their texts right to their noses.

I thought back to a Saturday morning Shabbat service I'd attended a few years previous. There people had walked around, conversing, teasing each other, even as the service continued. At certain points they would all sing out a responsory to the cantor's call, then return to reading or talking. I had put down the liturgy I couldn't follow anyway and watched the amazing unison of communal worship and anarchy, everyone joining at the right time and enjoying each other the whole time. One man, however, stood off in a side aisle with the text, swaying side to side, then bowing excitedly forward, alone and completely consumed with saying the words spilling out before him. My host had leaned to whisper in my ear. "He's concentrating. It helps him focus, and the words are so rich. They have him, see." The man had begun swaying again, like the hand-held prayer turnstiles that Tibetans spin for hours when praying.

"This is a yeshiva," the rabbi whispered. How I heard him under the noise baffled me. "Here we learn from the Torah. There is nothing more important in the world." A couple of men lay down their books and replaced them with styrofoam cups of coffee. They never halted their discussion.

We left the study center and ate a late lunch in the meat dining room (as distinguished from the milk dining room. Milk and meat cannot be mixed in kosher kitchens.) Over a plate of spaghetti I was introduced to David, an Irish-born sojourner who was working and studying at the yeshiva in preparation for the exams that would allow him to convert to Orthodox Judaism. "Sure you can stay and help. It'll be welcomed with all we've got to finish by Pesach." I rinsed my plate, and he picked up a scrub brush. "Would you mind starting with these two trash cans?"

So it was that I entered Diaspora Yeshiva Toras Israel, working during the day and attending classes at night. The yeshiva had been established especially for people from the United States who wanted to come to the land of Israel for study and who had either grown up outside of a religious context or had broken with the tradition. Some rose as early as I did, and as I began picking up garbage and weeding flower beds I could hear them davening through the opened window above me, praying in the morning service.

On most mornings I washed my head and face in a sink and began to work with the sun. The cold and early light refreshed me more than any shower could have. It felt good to be in a place for more than a few days and to work in solitude so early in the day. Knowing that what I did had to be done before Passover could be celebrated rendered the most laborious of tasks bearable. The beginning of the day was always joyful and clean there.

One morning I was busy hacking at a huge vine that had become embedded in a gateway and threatened to tear apart the stones around which it ran. In the quiet little street that divided the yeshiva campus in two a taxi pulled up. The driver rolled down his window.

"Hey, can you tell me where Dormition Abbey is?" The Benedictine abbey which supposedly houses the sleeping body of the Virgin Mary was only a few streets down from where I stood and could be seen on the skyline. As I began to give directions, a student of the yeshiva walked by.

"I wouldn't do that if I were you!" he growled under his breath as he passed me. I looked up at him. "I wouldn't do that if I were you," he repeated. "It's against the rules."

"Don't worry, anyway, they're tourists, they're Christians," the taxi driver said. I looked again at the yeshiva student without understanding what he was talking about. I wanted to give lost people directions. He glared at me.

"It's against the rules to show anyone where to worship idols!" he warned. Past conversations about Christianity registered in my mind. I could feel irritation growing within me. I met his gaze and he turned in a huff, striding down the street. I watched him until he disappeared and then returned to the driver.

"It's just to the left, you can see it there," I said. "The quiet is beautiful inside, and the Mass."

"Thanks," the driver smirked. I went back to cutting as the taxi pulled away.

In the kitchen before breakfast the student confronted me again. "It's against the rules to show people the place of idol worship. It's a violation of the covenant God asks us to keep."

I looked at him. There was nothing to say. If that was the rule then I had broken it and of free choice. He knew I was Christian and undoubtedly wondered what in God's name I was doing in his yeshiva.

I often wondered the same. In as much as I loved and respected the environment of worship and study, negative aspects of life in the community grew more and more pronounced as my stay extended. What I had first romanticized as a remarkable religious community showed itself as an overgrown family of squabblers. Students fussed endlessly at each other. Divided along an age gap, the younger found the older to be intolerable old men, disenchanted with life through failure in work or marriage who had resorted to a fundamentalist religious devotion that promised to solve all their problems. The younger were seen as lazy and irreverent, problem kids who had been whisked away by their parents for the price of a plane ticket to Israel from the United States. Both were sometimes completely just analyses, but were frequently carried to extremes in the actions of one group to another. Once when working in the kitchen I stepped out to find someone that could light the stove for me. Gentiles cannot light the fire in a kosher kitchen, and I asked the first student I saw if he would help.

"If you don't mind," I said. "If not, I can ask somebody else."

"Well, do want me to help or not?" he scolded, still bleary eyed from having just awakened. We walked in silence to the kitchen and he lit the stove indignantly.

"What's wrong with him?" David asked after he left. He began to scramble eggs over the flame.

"He just blew up when I asked if he'd help."

"Yeah, that one, he won't talk to young people."

"What do you mean?" The idea was so simplistic I took it as a joke.

"I mean, he hates talking to kids. I wish he hated talking to me. He asked another student how old he was once, and then he said, 'Oh, you're younger than me, that's it for talking.' And when the other guy asked what he meant, he wouldn't even look at him or answer. Some kind of sadness people live with."

The same frustrated intolerance showed up frequently. Older students yelled at the younger for adopting stray animals and keeping them in the yeshiva's apartments. The younger ridiculed the older for their unquestioning acceptance of all the teachings and a sickening devotion to the head rabbis. At meals the first in line would take enormous helpings without consideration of the inevitable shortage awaiting the latecomers. Those left with less to fill their plates complained to the cooks that not enough care had been taken to provide for them. Dinner table conversation would degenerate into boasts about the prestige of carrying a gun, the devotion to a God of patriotism to which it witnessed, and jokes abounded about the danger of letting your wife "get a hold of it." The issue of what it takes to be a good wife was a constant topic of debate as many of the older men had come to the yeshiva in order to make a match. To spite their pious desire, the younger generation brandished stories of sexual exploits, an attack on the older group's frustrated waiting and claim on superior knowledge.

Issues of justice, when discussed, were argued on grounds of ethnic and religious identity. Advocates of human rights and democracy were ridiculed as proponents of secular gentile and therefore intrinsically perverse systems of thought and governance. As time wore on I became aware that few in the yeshiva held the Israeli political system in very high regard. Many feared spying and conspiracies against religious groups such as their own. They considered the secular state an abomination. If God was finally fulfilling the ancient and prophetic promise of restoring the land of Canaan to the people of Israel, it was in their view incumbent upon them to adhere to the dictates of the Torah. The Law of God defined the people of God by their actions and intentions, and the Law of God was perfect, a revelation of God to humanity. Secular law, as a replacement for the old biblical code, blasphemed by implicitly denying divine rule. In their view, a religious court should govern the people according to their strict and literal interpretation of the Law.

This religious idea of government was inseparable from the concept of land ownership. The land of Palestine was by divine order theirs and should be taken without fear or regard to costs. Many of those I met at the yeshiva, especially the teachers, were illegal settlers in areas of East Jerusalem and the West Bank reserved for Arab-Israelis. Their children rode to religious school every day on a bus covered in bulletproof glass, all in the name of the love of God. Although they feared changes toward a more liberal government, a tacit agreement seemed to exist between Israeli politicians and ultra-orthodox activists. Though nominally barred from settling in Palestinian territory, Jewish Israeli settlements grew rapidly. Many of the settlers were strongly religious and associated with yeshivas. The Israeli government paid a monthly stipend to students who devoted themselves to study in yeshivas, regardless of age. Some men spent their entire lives supporting large families just by studying. I often wondered if such practices were not a continuation of early Zionist efforts to populate Palestine with a majority of thoroughly patriotic settlers in the name of religious devotion.

Without question, Arab-Israelis were considered to be second-rate citizens, even undeserving citizens, of the state. In the yeshiva, calling another "goyim-lover" served as an insult bandied about with vindictive flare. A "goyim" is a gentile, and the phrase was used in much the same way that whites in the United States have denigrated each other with the term "nigger-lover." Racism and ethnocentrism functioned on many levels, however. As many Ethiopians sought to immigrate into Israel out of religious devotion and to flee political persecution and violence, some at the yeshiva found it necessary to question the validity of the Ethiopians' claim to Jewish ethnic and religious heritage. Practitioners of Conservative or Reform Judaism were considered just as sacrilegious and traitorous as secular Jews. The rabbi that first greeted me into the yeshiva once began to show me photographs of a demonstration he had helped orchestrate. "We gathered yeshiva students together from all over the city and helped them make these signs," he said. I could tell the protest had been held at the Wailing Wall and that a huge crowd had turned out in support of the rabbi's side, but I could not tell what they had gathered to advocate. Our conversation was interrupted, and I turned to ask another student. He looked away and then became angry.

"I'll tell you," he said. "News came that a group of rabbis from the U.S. were coming to pray at the Temple Wall. Some of them were women and they were also going to be praying, wearing phylacteries and prayer shawls, which only men do in our tradition. But they were reformed.

"So these rabbis organized boys to stand between the Wall and the reformed rabbis while they prayed. They yelled at them. Some of them yelled that they should go back to Auschwitz with their ancestors for mistreating religion that way." He looked at me and turned away. "This place is so fucked up," he muttered and walked off.

It was as if a little group of people were drawing

a line around themselves, singling themselves from all other people and ways of thinking. From conversations throughout the month, I came to understand that not only the orthodox adherents were separating themselves. Orthodox practitioners scathingly criticized conservative and reformed Jews; the latter two seemed to shun, and almost fearfully so, the orthodox when passing one another in the street. Journalists, writing from an apparently secular perspective, found easy scapegoats in the backward ideas and demonstration antics of orthodox youth. Stories abounded of the Israeli government's own self-division. The example most frequently cited recounted the inaction of the bodyguards when Nobel Peace Prize Laureate and President Yitzak Rabin was assassinated. Israel was a house divided, and I was becoming increasingly baffled by the endless volleys of criticism and anger filling every conversation. The yeshiva was an island in a tiny archipelago. I was ready to leave.

"Where are you headed, mate?" David asked in the kitchen the day before I left.

I paused, then answered simply, "Gaza."

He stopped sweeping for a moment and then resumed without much change in attitude. "It's a hard place, that. Dirty. Reminded me of India and places such as that."

"You've been there?"

"Yup, maybe 2 or 3 years ago." He swept a few strokes before continuing. "But I couldn't go now." He peered up at his kipah. "Besides what everybody here'd think."

I leaned over the kitchen counter and looked at him across the dining room floor. "David, do you ever doubt yourself being here and converting? Everyday there's something for you to criticize."

"Hey, mate... it's God what brought me here and I'll stay till I go. Like you said when you came."

I went back to scrubbing the dishes.

Yet I would err gravely if I recorded only examples of conflict from my time in Israel. Despite my desire to be free from the frustration of so complex and alienating a milieu as Jerusalem, I left an immense joy when I crossed the southern border into autonomous Palestinian Territory in Gaza. In Israel, one cannot walk far in any direction without meeting some new view of beauty, a turn in a building or an alley, shadows crawling across a mountain with the rising day. Beauty is inescapable there. Tel Aviv is restful in its unpronounced modernity and quotidian pace. Haifa, despite its industrial character, is white as scorched bone and green from scrub and pine trees on Mount Carmel, the colors enunciated sharply by the hard blue of the Mediterranean sea and sky. Jerusalem has grown out of its own hills. Its boulevards funnel into the hidden silent streets of the Old City, winding and dark and lonely as caverns until they surface into plazas where vendors bask in sunlight. And these are only the cities. On a long bus ride from Jerusalem to the Galilee and the city of Safed, I dropped down through the Judean Mountains and traveled north along the Jordan River. The bus traveled through a corridor, the Jordan Mountains impassive on the right beyond the little river, the Judean hills on the left. For hours I watched the slow transformation of those hills from smooth, coned forms of the desert, like golden silk, to broken red mountains. They slowly began to support green growth and eroded into the low maternal mountains bearing down on the shores of the Sea of Galilee.

The country expresses the ability of its people to develop and preserve the land's innate beauty. The impressions this leaves a visitor are those of wisdom and controlled strength. Israel has been able to construct itself without destroying its land in the process. It has become tied to it and now grows out of it, as Jerusalem grows out of white bone rock.

I grew angry as I passed through Israel, in part due to disillusionment. I rarely found the justice and unity I had envisioned based on friendships in the United States and readings. The collision of an unjust history with natural beauty is what rendered my time there so difficult, but it also attracted me to the land. As in the United States—and perhaps in all nations born of a European colonial mentality—the natural grace of the country conflicted with the land's recent history. I drive through western North Carolina and long to live in the mountains, as do thousands of others. We constitute a continued invasion. How could I live in the southern Appalachians knowing my cultural complicity in the continued alienation of the Catawba and Cherokee people from their ancestral land? I bought groceries and a bus ticket to see the Galilee. But how could I exult in the grandeur of those gentle mountains after economically supporting, regardless of how small the degree, the continued oppression of indigenous Palestinians? And yet I did.

And I drew strength from the determination of the Israelis. My hand ran lightly along the freshly hewn stone of a Jerusalem wall; I could feel the almost fatalistic resolve to build a life as free as possible from a history of persecution and outsider status. The knotty trees bordering residential streets in Tel Aviv witness to the fight to make a home despite a world of indifference and accusations. I do not admire the wrongs committed in the name of liberty in Israel anymore than I do in the United States. I detest the blind factionalism that dominates so much thought and conversation in Israel and especially in Jerusalem. But the question of whether or not Israelis should be in Palestine is as moot as debating keeping Euro- and Afro-Americans in the Americas. Though I must qualify my praise of Israel where qualification is needed, I am also free to testify to the remarkable strength of the people. The land, urban and rural, communicated their purpose to me daily. It ironically empowered me to see and then to rebuke less than noble situations and practices. But in spite of my indignation, admiration and indeed love persists in me for this land.

At the yeshiva I always wore a stocking cap out of respect for the practice of humbling oneself before God by keeping the head covered. March in Jerusalem is not far removed from winter and can be decidedly cold. But some afternoons warmed to the point of disagreeing with my wool cap and I spent a good deal of time scratching and sweating rather than weeding and scrubbing. An older rebbe, come fairly new to the community, approached me one day. He had a habit of depositing his daily gripes with me, complaining about such-and-such a person or about such-and-such a group, or about both. Sometimes he lectured about the disgrace of Christianity in the world, "But not about you, you understand? I know you think differently." Though he cared for me and taught me enormously, I found his presence sometimes irritating. As he hobbled over I bore down on dried spaghetti clinging to a pot.

"Scott," he called quietly. He was always a bit self-conscious when approaching anyone or broaching any topic, a trait that endeared him to many. I looked up.

"Rebbe?"

"Look," he said, stepping around the counter and into the kitchen. "I've been watching you work. I wanted to thank you for always wearing your cap. It's appreciated by us," he reflected for a moment and chuckled, "even by us the unappreciative." I laughed a little too and looked back at the sink. "But you've got to be, I mean..." He fumbled for words and looked away self-consciously, then reached in his pocket and stuffed a little black cloth in my hand. As he turned and started quickly out the door, he explained. "I mean, it's got to get hot out there some days. Anyway, you keep it."

I opened my hand to a little black skullcap. Long white hairs and some short ones clung to the fabric. Little smears of mud circled the crown. I washed it three times thoroughly before the water running through it maintained its clarity. I only wore it a few times for Shabbat services and meals where stocking caps seemed too out of place. Otherwise I guarded my cap, unable to completely identify myself with a community with whom my argument was growing. But I kept it in my back pocket always until I crossed into Gaza.

On the afternoon of my first Friday at the yeshiva, David came up to me. I was kneeling on slabs of cut stone and pulling weeds from their teeth. Little spines stuck me and caused my fingertips to swell.

"That's good, mate," he said.

"Thanks."

"No, I mean, you can stop now. Time to shower up and get ready for Shabbat. You got anything to wear tonight?"

"Just what you've seen me in these past few days," I smiled. Tiny spiked weeds clung to my shirt and smeared into green stains here and there. He looked me over.

"Right. Well. Come along then, we'll see if we can't find something to fix us up."

In his room above the dining hall David scrounged around for my Shabbat suit and shortly produced a slightly tight white Oxford shirt, a green and red striped tie, and a black overcoat. "You can just wear your pants and shoes as usual," he advised. "So we'll see you up in the study room tonight near 6, and then if you want some of us is going across town to a big dinner hosted by a rabbi. So come along if you like. Everyone'd like you to go, and you'll like the rabbi well, I think."

When I showed up in the overcoat for prayers that night, he was impressed with his fashion skills. The garden boy had been transformed. "Looking nice, mate," he murmured.

I consider my trip to Israel to have begun in India a few months before. After I'd worked for a few weeks with Sister Jessi in her grassroots schools around Bodh Gaya, she received an invitation to visit her native Kerala in the south of the country. A vipassanna meditation retreat led by Westerners was to be held in the town and its dates coincided exactly with the time I had left before going on to my next month of work in western Gujarat. Just before entering the ten days of silent breathing meditation I was introduced to Seth Castleman, another U.S. American traveling and working in a pioneer school near Lucknow, northeast of Bodh Gaya. We found dinner together and fell to talking about our religious traditions. Seth told the story of his break with Judaism, about his frustration with the conflict between its practice and what he understood its potential to be. His love of what was possible, of what surely was there, led him to go away from the faith of his childhood in search of the realization of its spirit elsewhere. He came to Buddhist practice and ironically found through it a growing understanding of the teachings of covenant and obedience that had before seemed antagonistic to his conception of God. The point, he explained, was not to know what God was. He compared the effort to trying to understand what a lover was. The important idea was not to know what, but to be with the beloved. After coming into this understanding, his struggles with the Law became an attempt to live more fully in the presence of God. He wrestled with Judaism and not against it. He reminded me of a rabbi who told me once that the Jewish idea of Heaven is to sit in the presence of God with all of the great scholars, arguing points of philosophy and law.

Seth had begun practicing Judaism again, and he questioned the retreat injunction not to use candles. In our introductory meeting, he posed the problem.

"Yes?" the moderator recognized the hand in the right wing.

"Is that rule absolute? Even, for instance, at about six on Friday nights?" Seth asked. After a brief discussion, the moderator smiled and promised to talk to him personally afterwards.

The question grew into a congregation. Others in the retreat approached the leaders about being involved in the Shabbat service. On the first Friday Seth kept his shaved head hidden under a pile of blankets that varied in height depending on the changing temperature. At dusk I saw him in a group ascending a staircase into a clean, well-lighted apartment. I later heard that the retreat leader had asked if he might attend as well.

"Bring your scissors," Seth agreed.

On the second Friday of the retreat, an open invitation was extended to the entire group. That evening perhaps twenty people crowded into the same little room that turned out to be the apartment of the retreat leader. Cushions had been placed in a circle on the floor. In the empty center, two candles and a few metal glasses appeared. Seth covered his head in a white crocheted kipah and closed his eyes. For a moment he relaxed. We were all still a little restless, trying to find space to lean against the walls. He waited for us to settle and then leaned forward.

"Tonight we'll use fruit juice and these cakes instead of wine and bread. It's what we found in the little store across the street. I hope no one will take exception to our improvisation."

"Of course, some of us are new to this and some are veterans." Seth glanced at the retreat leader and smiled to tease about his one week of experience. "But everyone is welcome here, and we are here together to welcome in the Shabbat. It's the traditional day in every week when Jews particularly concentrate on remembering God and God's gifts, and we can all use it as a time to pay special attention to the world around us and what we have received from it."

I sat in the doorway behind most people, and though I took juice and cakes at their appropriate times, I mostly concentrated on Seth. His freshly shaven head was nicked and shone vulnerably under the delicate white kipah. He was completely focused on the elements in the center of our circle. When the wine had to be poured, he helped hand out the yellow fruit-juice boxes that had already been opened so that no seal would be broken on the Sabbath. He explained every step as much to remind those familiar with the service of each moment's importance as to guide those of us in a new context. He stared at the candles melting onto the floor as we passed bread from hand to hand. The circle completed, we looked to him for the next step. For a moment he remained oblivious to our attention, then the weight of the pause woke him and he looked around, a bit startled.

"We should sing something," he said. It was more of a question than a directive. His mind was empty and he had no immediate song to offer. "Does anyone have a song they'd like to try?" Silence, a little laughter from the silence, and then a verse came to his memory. Seth murmured the first few words absently, not even really aware that he was pronouncing them. The sounds triggered a thought; someone in the back spoke them louder; another picked up the tune and began to sing. Seth joined the song and then others did, remembering their mothers in Montreal and Paris singing the same song one Friday decades ago. Clapping bounced between the floor and our ears; another stanza bridged the pause of forgetfulness; the night went on.

Through the night air in Jerusalem David and I crossed empty streets with three others from the yeshiva. Single cars slipped down main thoroughfares and one student asked, "Should we walk in the street?" We could hear another group yelling at open stores and passing vehicles 'Shabbis! Shabbis!' rebuking transgressors of the orthodox interpretation that driving is also a form of work on the day of rest. Despite the intolerance and self-righteousness of their ridicule, the weird silence of the evening made the situation surreal. The shouts were more like those of a party than a threat, kids rowdy with the headiness of a special night. The whole city seemed to have suddenly become depopulated but for us.

But when we arrived at the Rabbi Machowitz's home, I corrected my error. The city was not empty; it had filled the dining room we were about to try to enter. Squeezing past plastic folding chairs and children hyper with the commotion of the crowd, we made our way to the back and sat against a glass sliding door. Someone had cracked it open, and the chill outside tightened my back muscles as sweat moistened my armpits and waist.

I felt that we had come home. The walls were covered in proverbs and quotations calligraphied in Hebrew and English. 'Joy is a mitzphah,' one read.

Bottles of grape juice and wine were being circulated and all of our thin plastic cups were soon brimming. Conversations ended in half-sentence as men assumed voluntary silence to be broken by eating blessed bread yet to be distributed. Across from me a thin man with wispy white hair snoozed, started, and settled again. "See, everybody's welcome here at the Rabbi's," David whispered. "Even the drunks what's got nowhere to go. He understands, the Rabbi does." In the kitchen the hostess and her daughters scrambled to pull last dishes from the ovens. The rabbi stood to welcome everyone.

"First of all," he began, "you are all welcome." Scattered clapping was quickly hushed by the crowd. "My family, my daughters, my son, my wife, and myself, we all welcome you as we begin this Shabbat together.

"Please eat all you can. We want nothing left. But let's also remember those who are without, and not waste any of what God has given us in such greatness."

"Please remember also that there are many people here, in number and in kind. We want to be as patient and caring with each other as we can while we distribute the food to one another and while we speak to one another. As we go through the meal I will explain certain things, certain prayers and so forth, so that everyone will understand what is happening. I want for us all to understand the importance of what we are doing, and I ask that those of you that are well acquainted with the Shabbat meal and the things I say to simply be patient for those of us who have come up in another tradition or another way.

"And I ask especially that you all help me with singing, because there is a lot to be done tonight, and though I love singing I am terrible at it. So that you, our guests, will not leave, please make it easier on everyone by singing as loudly as you can. Good Shabbis everyone." And a resounding 'Good Shabbis!' thanked him in return.

A song of welcome was begun, calling everyone to put aside their concerns and fears and to welcome Shabbat and the new week it led to us. As we sang, the Rabbi's wife appeared carrying the four biggest loaves of bread I had ever seen to the center of the room. They were more than half the height of the Rabbi, perhaps four feet long each, and so thick in the middle that the knife's blade completely disappeared into the first loaf when the Rabbi began cutting. They were wrapped in a blue velvet cloth and stacked in pairs, back to back. The Rabbi took them from his wife and cradled them in his arms. He squinched his eyes shut and began rocking, rocking, and then sang out in a strained voice his thanks for these things that we were all to receive. Men in the group joined him and their swaying produced a choir of squeaking chairs, groaning under the shifting weight of religion and feasting. The prayer ended, and the Rabbi began cutting, hacking, tearing at the bread. His daughters surrounded him and they grabbed the torn pieces, throwing them on a silver platter. Once piled high the bread began to be passed, over heads and tables to the back recesses of the room, then across the room, crossing other platters piled high with mountains of bread diminishing in size with every chair passed over, through the room and out the door of the apartment to the crowd outside that couldn't fit in with us. We all held our bread, another brief prayer was said in thanks to encourage attentiveness to the bread we would soon enjoy, and then we ate. The room erupted in conversation, half of the crowd finally released from the vow of silence taken only a few minutes before. The feast ensued with trays of chicken, fish, and every sort of vegetable and cake following the same routes of the bread platters. I sat in the joyful chaos surrounded by students of the yeshiva and strangers. In those hours our political and religious arguments mattered little.

Later that night while returning to the yeshiva the student seated next to me would charade the acts of a terrorist bombing churches that we passed. We separated that evening on poor terms and never wholly healed the rift. But a week later we sat together again in the home of this same Rabbi from Connecticut. The Rabbi led the prayers and the student turned to me with a bottle of wine.

"Its top is still sealed, and I can't open it. Would you help me?" he asked. No creative act may be performed on the seventh day by an observant Jew. To do such is to slight God. On that day creating insinuates that God did not complete Creation and that humanity must help itself by finishing things. An unopened door must remain closed; a torn cloth must remain unsewn; there is no way to retrieve the contents from a sealed bottle. But a gentile must break some rule in recognition of his distance from the Law. My adversary could not drink, and I was the only one at the table able to help him.

I had found myself mired in petty religious disputes for a month. My search for saints had apparently been detoured by a misguided contact and then interrupted by a fateful offer to do volunteer work for a few weeks. Even the most liberal of students at the yeshiva had grown wary of my ideas. An offhand conversation with one about coexistence ended in his yelling at me, "We're at war, man! Arabs hate Jews and Jews hate Arabs!"

"But I know Jews and Arabs willing to work on living together! I talked to one of them for four hours one day in Haifa!" I countered in exasperation.

"Who gives a fuck about one person, man?! Okay, one person. One person! But 99% of Arabs hate Jews, and 99% of Jews hate Arabs! What the fuck are you talking about living together?!" he railed.

The student held a bottle of red wine and looked to me for a hand. "Unscrew the top, please, I can't break the seal without blaspheming God."

Later I would think again about how ridiculous and damaging all our conceptions of rightness and divinity can be.

But no malice showed in the student's eyes. It never occurred to me to hesitate. I took the bottle and filled my cup after his.

The Saints

By 1:30 the crowd had packed the square of the Franciscan Abbey to the point of immobility. Bodies rolled around each other like gumballs pushing down toward the dispenser's chute.

Over our heads squawked rows of loudspeakers

broadcasting the tinny chants of the brothers' high mass. Despite the volume, one had to stand right beside the stereo in order to hear what was being said. A cacophony of guitars, songs, people shouting, waving to each other, donkeys braying, and ice-cream vendors hawking popsicles in the chilly April afternoon crowded the air. How we would ever coherently walk down the hill and into the city without crushing hundreds of ourselves eluded me.

Then suddenly the crowd began to separate. A narrow avenue formed down its middle. Led by yellow flags carried by Palestinian Boy Scouts the Franciscans processed out of the church, the hems of their robes scratching the paving stones, continuing their psalms.

Automatically, with almost no direction, congregations began to join the parade, one by one, taking up their songs and marching toward Jerusalem from the Mount of Olives.

Palm branches waved in the air. I wandered through the crowd, walking beside one group, then falling back to follow another for a while. Everyone, everyone, seemed light and happy. No one rushed. One step was enough for every foot.

At one point I stepped out of the processional and stood on a low wall, watching the mixture of cultures pass by me. A congregation of German Protestants strumming familiar hymns on their guitars gave way to white robed French monastics, out of their cloisters for this one day, toting accordions and singing medieval folk songs. Then an Arabic group passed, dancing to the din of cymbals and floral arpeggios. And so Palm Sunday continued, one nation after another, sometimes accidentally singing the same tune at the same time, all walking together.

As we entered the Lion's Gate in the Arab Quarter of old East Jerusalem, Muslims lined the streets and cemetery walls, cheering us on, even sometimes joining their friends and conversing loudly as we passed under the gates.

Gaza City, The Gaza Strip, Palestine

5 April 1999 – 1 May 1999

In the city I found you,
All love, wrestling every stone.

I give you my words, my happiness.
Use it all for your freedom.

I give you everything
Except myself.

One morning I was lingering between jobs at Madraset Atfaluna, a school for deaf children in the Gaza Strip. Along with another volunteer I had been assigned the responsibility of producing the school's English language newsletter. I had been running circles through the building hunting down teachers for interviews and getting my directions mixed between Palestinian Sign Language and Arabic. The work's tempo had slowed and under the pretense of tracking down some necessary element for a minor job, I had begun to snoop around the second floor rooms. My curiosity pulled me easily past the exigencies of my conscience and I wandered from room to room, poking through bookshelves and studying posters in Arabic of how to tie shoelaces. I pulled out my camera and started greedily clicking shots.

As time passed my caution waned. Striding absently into the hallway I almost ran into two women, a teacher and a student. Surprised, they started and jumped back.

Thumb-to-chin, the student signed my name. Her eyes had warmed to a luminous excitement after being startled. *Right-hand-fingers-to-forehead,* she greeted me with a firm salute.

"Hey, Nemat, Aycha," I said, recovering my own calm and motioning the greeting as I spoke. "Okay, you caught me."

"And you caught us," Nemat laughed, signing our talk to include Aycha. "But it's break now, so you're doing nothing wrong. Except that you're off by yourself again and not with us down on the playground."

Aycha's thin hands quavered like fish in the air. Nemat laughed and Aycha grabbed her sides, rolling back on her heels and spilling across the wall in pleasure at her joke.

"Wait, wait, I didn't get it, what'd she say?" Losing your place in a three-language conversation can happen easily, and I didn't want to miss the punch line.

Nemat tried to assume a tone that made the joke her own. "She just asks why we need you to play." The teasing antagonism hit its target.

"More like wanting me there to talk. And talk and talk and talk," I jabbed. I molded my hands into a duck head and soundlessly quacked at Aycha while pointing at Nemat.

Without a comeback, Nemat tried to end the teasing before she fell behind in the score. She waved her hands in mock exasperation. "Okay, right. That's how you see me? Always talking? And what are you doing, always disappearing?"

"I am working on the newsletter. And taking pictures so that I can talk about Atfaluna when I'm back home." The evidence hanging around my neck whacked me in the stomach as I gesticulated, trying to get the sense of my words clearly to Aycha. She laughed at my confusion and rattled out paragraphs to Nemat.

"Yes, yes," Nemat signed. "You know," she said turning to me, "Aycha thinks you are making up nonsense. She says you were just hiding from us. And that you should practice your signing more. So you know what I think, Scott? I think you should come more to our class to learn Arabic and Palestinian signing."

"Certainly." I bowed sarcastically, then qualified my submission to their whims with a touch of spitefulness. "Just as soon as I finish *my work*."

"And what is more important than learning Palestinian signing to speak with the children? And learning Arabic to speak to me?" Aycha nodded her agreement to Nemat's self-translation. "Taking pictures for Americans? Will you talk about me in America?"

"How could I not?!" I buckled under the invisible weight of my growing log of Nemat memories.

"Good. You should not ever forget me or the children—"

"...But especially not you...?"

She smiled delightedly. "Scott, you will kill me with all this joking. You think you are so good—"

"And if I am not good, why talk to me?" I would prod the teasing as far as it could go. But Nemat detoured the conversation, and I acquiesced.

"I talk to you only to practice my English, and also because you need help to talk with the students."

"Okay, that's good, thank you for helping me." And it is true that no one else could have offered such diligent and enjoyable help in any situation. Aycha, who had been forgotten in the banter, stepped between us and wheeled to face Nemat.

"She says that if you are going to talk about us in America then you should have a picture of us. So that you will never forget us."

"And how could I forget you?"

In the picture, their faces blaze out happily. Nemat stoops to Aycha's height and they hug close together. Wisps of long black hair have escaped from under Aycha's head covering and cling to her long jaw line. Their scarves are pulled neatly and tightly across their foreheads and are swallowed by the neckline of blue woolen sweaters. White on white, the sheen of light on silk pulls twining vines of flowers into relief. If the covering were worn of their own choice, I would write that it was beautiful. The enthusiasm and courage of these two women, Aycha the student and her teacher Nemat, spring out from the fabric's serene constriction.

Though I tried always to distance myself from preconceptions when entering a new month of journeying, I had not anticipated the joyful power that Aycha and Nemat incarnated. Generic memories of Amnesty International reports from Islamic cultures had eliminated any consideration that women might play a prominent role during my stay in Gaza. Almost every day there offered a lesson to the contrary of my assumption. But their joy surprised me just as much as their assertiveness.

When I told friends and professors that I had been offered the chance to visit the Gaza Strip, I was almost always met by cautionary congratulations. In the West we retain memories of Gaza from news blurbs during the *intifada*. Kids hurled stones at soldiers. Tanks lumbered through streets and demolished buildings. The period of popular uprising and revolt was certainly a time of terror and constant danger, but it constitutes a relatively short period in the history of Gaza and the Palestinian people. "Remember that you've got one life to live—give it well, okay?" The advice came from a seasoned traveler and dedicated advocate for justice and human rights, and I didn't take the wisdom lightly. It was rather an honor that someone thought that I might be willing to render up my spirit to a cause greater than my exotic trip.

Throughout my month's stay in Haifa and Jerusalem, my previous idea of Gaza was cultivated despite my disillusionment with Israel. Though I sided more and more adamantly with the Palestinians as the weeks progressed, my view of Gaza did not improve. Headlines in English dailies announced United Nations studies that revealed a higher incidence of human rights abuses in Palestinian administered territories than in Israel. On a walk with a Jewish acquaintance in Jerusalem we stepped into a shop owned by an Arab Israeli. "What are you doing with a Jew?" he asked heatedly after our introduction. "Do you know what they did to us? Do you know what they did?" He began pulling down accounts of the 1948 war and flipped to photographs of dead children and toppled houses, shoving them in our faces and asking why we had come into his store. My partner attempted a plea for co-existence. He was met first with shocked silence, then with an expulsion. "Do not come back, do not come back into my store! Never, never, never!"

On the border between Israel and the Gaza Strip, I had peered past fences to see into the future. Anticipating poverty equaling India and cysts of violence ready to erupt had sharpened my attention, and I studied the terrain. I would be going through those gates, and then I would be in Gaza for a month.

"It's actually over there," my contact said. He pointed to the right of the fences. "You're looking back into a corner of Israel that way." Dr. Dean and Mrs. Donna Fitzgerald served in the Atli Hospital in downtown Gaza. They had picked me up in a bus station south of Tel Aviv. After treating me to a Big Mac, we made the short drive to the border. Dr. Fitzgerald pulled a metal bar from behind the seat and locked the gearshift and the accelerator to the steering wheel. The lifeless parking lot became a car thief's Wal-Mart at night, he joked.

We passed easily through Israeli security and walked a few hundred yards towards the Palestinian gate. The avenue was empty. We alone broke the flat plane of the asphalt. "Over there," Dr. Fitzgerald motioned to his left, "is the chute that the Palestinians have to pass through. U.S. passport, VIP security check. But the Palestinians have to walk through that chute," the pre-fab structure looked like an empty warehouse extending hundreds of yards, "to be checked. And they really get checked. Those guards ask every question possible and go through every bit of luggage.

I think it may be more their job to make coming in and out of Gaza hell than to actually check for weapons and contraband. But you can bet they're doing that too."

Mrs. Fitzgerald waved her passport at the Palestinian gate and we ambled through unpestered. A weathered Buick two-door sedan awaited us. Dr. Fitzgerald unfastened another wheel lock and pulled out into the vacant highway. "There you go," Mrs. Fitzgerald said. From a double-sized billboard Yassir Arafat beamed through his scraggly beard at us and all other very welcome guests.

Throughout the drive I waited for something to happen. Nothing did. One could not arrive in Gaza at a more peaceful time than three o'clock. Mid-afternoon is reserved for siestas and ends with the call to prayer at five. "It'll get busier," they promised as we slid through noiseless streets.

The peace that filled the city never abandoned it, not even on the most raucous of mornings when mule-drawn carts tangled and blocked traffic. The people were patient with each other. Bougainvillea, serving as a beautifying fence with its hidden barbs, climbed along the splintering rebar and virgin concrete of unfinished buildings. The muezzin's call sometimes seemed to be more of a community joke, like a younger sibling jumping on everyone's bed, than an interruption. I felt safer in Gaza City than I had anywhere else, monasteries in France aside. My entry into Gaza put the lie to my previous ideas of the city and its people. Only when entering Jerusalem, in the Palm Sunday Processional under the surveillance of the Palestinian Boy Scouts, did I feel more at ease.

"What is his name?" Gerry Shawa introduced me to a handful of primary students to begin my first day at Atfaluna School for the Deaf. Before its founding a few years ago, no formal schooling was available to deaf children in Gaza. Because the territory is so cloistered from the rest of the world, genetic deafness occurs at a high rate. Until the teachers at Atfaluna began to instruct a systematized Palestinian Sign Language, the deaf in one neighborhood would be unable to communicate with others in adjoining quarters. A small group clustered around us, probing my face with alert eyes, then timidly guessing at what my sign name might be.

"No, no—he doesn't have a name," Mrs. Shawa corrected. "Give him one. What is his name?"

Like a flock of pigeons sweeping near us, dozens of deft hands immediately flew into action. Each threw ideas into the air as inspiration struck. The school's directress was no longer introducing us. The pupils had begun to initiate me.

Later in the day a student of eleven or twelve came up to me, eyes blazing out assertively under her covered hair. *What is your name?* she signed.

Thumb-rubbing-dimple-chin, I replied. After a few hours of incessant practice I was starting to answer with some minimal grace, actually placing my thumb on my chin rather than thumping myself in the teeth. But then she rushed into a long discourse that lost me after two signs. I waved her off in imitation of an air traffic controller unready for the next Boeing 747.

"Sorry, I didn't understand." She grabbed a marker

and began to write in English.

"OK. My name is Aycha. How long will you be at Atfaluna?"

"3 weeks," I scribbled back.

Her body rocked slightly with excitement and adolescent self-consciousness. *Welcome,* she smiled, touching her forehead. Then she motioned toward me confidently, *I will teach you, I will teach you.*

When I came to Atfaluna to observe the workings of the school through volunteering, I assumed that after picking up a few basic signs language difficulties would be eased. When people need to communicate they find a way, and I was willing to rely on improvisation. It had served me more than adequately and with ample attendant happiness since my time in Thailand. But the forthrightness of Aycha spoke clearly to more than just the need to pick up the local lingo while in town. In our first meeting, her excitement showed me her desire to welcome me to her school. But I felt that she also wanted to join me to Atfaluna's body, to the life of the students, though she may not have thought of it in such explicit terms. Inseparable from the force with which she opened the door was the expectation that I would step through it. I was being asked to do my part in learning equal to her enthusiasm for teaching.

Whether walking through the halls or assisting in classes, if ever communication broke down between a student and myself, this same desire arose immediately to remedy the situation. The right palm would go up blank, clearing the mind and calling for attention. Then the explanation, usually arduous and coupled with impatience and unending humor, would ensue. The underlying message could be read in every line of the hand: *You don't understand our language; you are here with us; we will help you learn.*

Coming into a new culture can sometimes equal stepping into a concert hall the moment before the *Ode to Joy* surges over the audience. But all of the symphonic movements in my first day at Atfaluna— the overwhelming confidence of even the youngest child; the care of the teachers; the determination of Gerry Shawa and her co-founders to keep the school running since its conception; the joyful impatience of every student trying to teach me; the energy in the classrooms—only describe the main motif: an attempt to pull me into *their* world. Touring through Atfaluna, one cannot help but pass along the periphery of what happens within the school. But once met, the students will in all earnestness try to bring the visitor into the heart of their days.

In Palestine, strangers and friends alike receive endless handshakes, greeted constantly with, "You are welcome, you are welcome." The same is true of the students at Madraset Atfaluna, but at an even higher level of engagement. One can speak regarding issues of human dignity or loneliness concerning deafness, but the central question revolves around an awareness of the difference between worlds. I, hearing and U.S. American, was utterly foreign at Atfaluna. But they, deaf, Palestinian, and eager, would have me and urged me into their circle.

On my first day at Atfaluna I met briefly with the directress, Gerry Shawa. My arrival, although previously arranged, was something of an interruption in her schedule. A group of tourists in Israel had dipped into Gaza for the day and wanted to visit the school. The demands of seeking funding were vital to the school's existence and she took every chance offered to ask for financial help. Like most NGO directors I met, she dreamed of being free of the economics of doing good in order to get down to the business of actually doing it. "Sometimes I wonder if my job is to direct or to host," she smirked while shuffling papers on her desk. A printed e-mail with a timetable had disappeared. She left her preoccupations and joined me for a cup of Turkish coffee.

"We'll arrange another time to sit and discuss the history of the place," she began. "For now I'll arrange you to be paired with a teacher—there are some here who really are excellent in English—and you can assist him or her in whatever most needs to be done. It'll give you a good view of the school through a regular routine of classes. And when I come up with something in particular that you might be able to help me on, I'll find you. Feel welcome here."

I did, I told her, and even more than the firm hospitality of Turkish coffee on an empty stomach, I expressed my appreciation for her informal U.S. American style and accent. Its familiarity relaxed me after half a year abroad.

"Well, I'm from Chicago. It's hard to shake. And it'll be nice for me to relax in a conversation—all the unspoken understandings we share culturally and linguistically, you know? You must know," she said to herself, "after all the continent leaping you've been doing."

We downed our drinks, and she showed me briefly

through the school, introducing me to the administration and to teachers in the hall. We walked into a wide classroom illumined by four tall windows that let in the blue sky. Two semicircular tables bracketed the open floor. Young students crowded around the two teachers manning their respective stations, prodding each other and flitting signs, swatting at hands they thought expressed incorrect theses. One girl began tickling a boy who had waxed on too long in order to disrupt his thought and talk. The teachers lifted their heads as we walked in and the students whirled around. They giggled and poked at each other when they saw us, wondering and asking who this grinning fool with the directress was.

"This is Nemat," Mrs. Shawa introduced me to the teacher seated at the far end of the room. She moved across to the desks and I followed. "Nemat is one of our outstanding teachers. She's here teaching math and religion, and then she gives classes in English and American Sign Language for the older students upstairs as well." Nemat had studied in a higher education program conducted in English by Marquette University in the Gaza Strip. She shook my hand and welcomed me by introducing me to her students. *He'll be with us for...* "How long will you be with us?" she asked, dropping her signs. Her students looked confused and then lunged across the table. They pulled on her sleeve and signed frantically.

"Two and a half, maybe three weeks," I answered, but she had already turned from me back to the students.

"Wait just a moment," she apologized with a laugh. *Four*, I saw her insist with extended fingers, then continued in signs that might have been shadow puppet formations for all I knew. The children settled and chatted to themselves, slapping and pulling, touching, touching, touching.

"Sorry." She returned to me with an enormous smile. "I dropped a sentence and they wanted me to complete it. You are here for four weeks? I mean three? Maybe you will learn Palestinian signing by then. Do you know American Sign Language already?"

I did not, and she asked why I was at Atfaluna if I had never worked with the deaf before. The explanation wound through the Far East before ending. Her eyes opened quizzically. She lowered them and smiled widely again. There was a great happiness in her.

"You have seen all these things? Then you must work with me every day, and I will teach you Palestinian sign language. You can tell me about everywhere you have been. I would love to see India. I have always wanted to see Jerusalem."

"You have never been to Jerusalem?" I asked. She chuckled at my innocence. She had never been to Jerusalem; she had never been out of the Gaza Strip. Her grandmother told stories of their former home near Tel Aviv and Yaffo, but she had never been.

"I learned English so well from the teachers at the Marquette program. You will see, the university years are very important in a person's life, no? And mine were in English with American university professors. So I am more American than I am Palestinian, even through I have never left Gaza." She shied with slight embarrassment and then laughed at my skepticism. "No, you will see," she insisted in a tone meant to convince me of her wisdom.

Nemat and I talked incessantly for the next week. I followed her in her daily routine. While she taught I noted the students' behavior, the room, the lesson, and while the students worked on exercises we talked about Gaza, the school, the students' backgrounds. My notebooks filled with Arabic lessons. One day I walked in late and a seventh chair had been added to the usual half-circle of six. My seven-year old neighbor smiled up at me and patted the empty seat, then turned assiduously back to his work.

I had become as much of a student as the others, and the temptation to speak English with an international vagabond and native speaker proved too much for Nemat. I assisted her on a few occasions, correcting spelling assignments in English and simple Arabic. A few times I taught her English class when she had to make house visits to absentees. But more often we would start conversing to the neglect of the more permanent students. We would talk on about Islam and Christianity or U.S. American favoritism in the Israeli-Palestinian conflict. One day she quoted a Palestinian proverb: "Endless talk about religion and politics ends more friendships." Her tone was mocking and not prophetic. Our minds had met and we drew all we could from each other, always sparring as we went. The class would grow restless and begin insisting that we either recommence the lesson or translate the conversation. Never before or since have I witnessed students begging so for work.

But our conversations rarely returned to the subject of my trip, and this became a point of frustration for Nemat. She nagged me about having a closed personality, and I retorted that she certainly had never received that accusation in her life. She frequently emphasized the reticence of other female teachers towards me and the men in the school. "Arabic women are not supposed to talk so much as I do," she bragged, "but you see that I do not care about what they think and say."

Her bravery in the face of social consternation raised concerns in me. "Would it be better if we cared?"

"No. Would you let somebody tell you who to talk to? I know how you think, I know it is natural for you to talk to me as you talk to Ehab and the other men, and the way you talk to Dennis. You see, I told you that I was more American than Palestinian."

But she did feel pressure from other opinions. I was invited, along with another volunteer and a good friend of Nemat's family who taught at Atfaluna as well, to visit her family's home one evening. I appreciated her nod to tradition if only because it eased the confusion I felt as a guest. I didn't know if talking in one situation was better than in another or how grievous a crime our conversation might be. A deliberate invitation allowed us the space to interact with minimized social constraint.

On the way we stopped on a steep hill by a corner market and bought a three-tiered box of candies. Christmas could not have made her happier. "This, you should not have done it. *Shuckran*," she thanked us and carried it away to set out on a silver platter. Emptied green and orange cellophane blew across the coffee table as we reached for more butterscotch.

That evening never produced the conversation she had hoped to have. The sitting room filled with brothers and friends and then a huge meal of kebabs, roasted and fresh vegetables, soups, pizza. As the daughter she was hostess and as guest I was meant to talk, but she never had the chance to join a conversation for any substantial length of time. At the evening's end her younger brother Ahed insisted that we meet again to continue talking about U.S. American life and religious ideas. Our talk had excited him, and he was eager. But Nemat showed frustration. "If I were a man," she muttered. "I could talk when I wanted and go outside of Gaza alone."

"You have to be escorted?" I asked. She glared at the grossness of my idiocy.

"Do you think alone is safe?" I could not tell if she were utterly sincere or sarcastic.

"Of all people, Nemat, you can."

When I had lived in Gaza City for a short time and had become acquainted with a few people, some of my new Palestinian friends expressed concern about my apartment. "Are you all right up there?" they would ask with some frequency. "Aren't you afraid of sleeping alone at night?"

After assuring them that I was perfectly fine sleeping alone and that I was in fact used to it, I sought out my contacts in the Gaza Strip, a group of U.S. American humanitarian workers that served as support staff for a hospital and a handful of schools, to ask them if I was missing something in the question.

"Did I understand what they were asking? Why were they so worried about me?" Having studied a little about Islam and Palestinian mores in preparation for my arrival, I felt certain they weren't offering me company for the night.

The group laughed. "It's just that average Palestinians have a hard time imagining anybody spending much time alone. Families are large and quarters are small. Most people have never spent a night of their lives in a room without somebody else around. The culture here is so social, and it's not just that people like being together—where would they go?"

The question's humor, though dark, betrays the answer's gravity. In the Gaza Strip, going where another is not can be difficult to do. The population is packed into something like a guarded reservation five miles wide and twenty-one miles long. Evicted from their homes and pushed off their land by the Israelis during the 1948 war for Israel's independence, Palestinians fled south to an area still controlled by Egypt. Enormous refugee camps sprang up but the dispossessed population was never returned to its homeland. The Palestinians had become a homeless people. Their camps slowly calcified into sprawling residential districts around Gaza and other southern cities bordering the Mediterranean Sea.

Though now an autonomous territory under the jurisdiction of the Palestinian Authority, the Gaza Strip is a living prison. To come in or out of the territory one must pass through Israeli security. For non-Palestinian visitors this involves little more than a long wait and suspicious or disdainful looks from the military police. For Palestinians, every entry and exit equals a full body search. Some talked to me about the migraines they suffered days afterward from the stress and humiliation they feel when they are ushered into one of the long row of stalls. Even travelers using the new Palestinian International Airport in

Raffah must go through an Israeli security check and customs regardless of their destination. The Gazan fishing and shipping industries should be profitable because of the territory's uninterrupted shoreline, but Israeli ships patrol the maritime border five miles from the coast and can shoot at any vessels attempting to pass that line. Passage in and out of the Gaza Strip and all international Palestinian trade are controlled by Israel. Many people have never left the territory, though their grandparents still recount stories describing life in their lost homeland. The memory of their loss at the hands of the young Israeli state will be continued long after first generation refugees are silenced.

The density of the population renders every act in Gaza public. If a family begins to celebrate, the neighborhood is sure to know about it quickly and may even be invited to join the fête. When I arrived in early April the marriage season was just beginning. I would lie awake for hours listening to pipers winding their way through streets to the huge bachelor parties taking place on every block for miles around. Shots would be fired and fireworks crashed crazily in the empty air. My apartment was situated in a United Nations compound with a hospital on one side and a large cemetery on the left. The white housing for the dead and healing buffered me from the parades and block parties. Whenever fireworks jumped the fence and fizzled to join tombstones, I felt as if the compound were under siege.

One night a knock came at my door. I lay quietly and listened for some indication of who it was. Often visitors would wander up from other apartments or the Gaza Deaf Club on the ground level. Many of the teachers and students with whom I worked frequented the Club. They would come by for a visit, but not having been raised in the social climate of Arabic Palestine, I would sometimes keep all of the lights off and act as if I were sleeping or out.

"Isn't Scott here?" they would ask each other. Someone would call down to another apartment.

"Hey, is Scott there?"

"Well, I thought I saw him earlier." The voice would usually be that of Dennis Walker, one of the humanitarian workers from the United States. His family's apartment was a story below and just opposite mine, across a small porch. "But he could've gone out, or have gone to sleep. Knock again, and if he's not there I'd leave him be." His Arabic left his mouth smoothly until it snagged on a moment of lost confidence and indecision. Human beings would live in greater harmony if there were more Dennis Walkers to mediate our affairs. For this and other reasons, Dennis became a close friend during my stay in Gaza City, a fellow member of the International Community of Introverts.

The knock came again. I lay still, listening for footsteps to descend the noisy metal stairs. Then a voice joined the next round of knocking.

"Scott? Scott. It's Dennis. If you're awake, open up."

I jumped off the couch and stumbled over a low table in the dark. I was nursing my shin when I opened the door. "Hey, what's up?"

"Hey, were you sleeping? I'm sorry if I woke you —"

"No, no," I grinned.

"Listen, there's a party across the wall on our block we've been invited to. I thought you might want to go. The chicken vendor down the street told me that we'd be very welcomed."

"It's the chicken shop owner's party? What kind of a party?" I asked. "Is this something you want to do?" It was almost eleven.

"Listen, it's his brother's wedding day tomorrow and this is the bachelor party. So about half of the male population in Gaza City is there, and the other half is on the way. I've been to a thousand of these and nobody's going to know if we came or not. We'll be lost in the crowd—well, you'll probably be remembered by a few people." He nodded at my frazzled blond hair. "But I think you might like it. We don't even have to go over there, we'll just go over to the wall and look over."

I grabbed my shoes and pulled on a sweatshirt, and we ran down the stairs toward the wall. I hadn't realized the chicken man was so popular. Fireworks spat up into the air in frenzied succession.

"Where is this thing?" I asked. The lights were coming from a normally nondescript lot. "Are those gun shots?"

"They're blanks," he laughed as we turned the corner. As we walked along the brick wall its height lowered until I could see over it easily. The crowd on the other side was immense. Men crowded a stage and fought playfully over a microphone, singing out of sync with a wailing tape. Half the crowd had the other half on their shoulders. Two or three held pistols which they fired at irregular intervals. Appropriately, the scene recalled childhood ambitions of world-record chicken fights. Everyone was dancing except for a few scattered groups of older men seated in chairs to the side.

"That's the groom in the green silk shirt," Dennis whispered, leaning towards me. The man he described, perhaps in his late twenties, rode on another's back and had joined hands with an elevated comrade. They waved their arms together like seaweed and spurred their mounts closer, further apart, in circles. "Do you recognize the one to his left?"

"No." The groom was in the middle of a crowd of hundreds. The music reverberated off the walls and apartment buildings around us. "Why are you whispering?"

"That one, over there," he said more loudly. "Do you see him? Know him? He sells the chickens, we met him the other day."

"Got him. I couldn't recognize him at first without the blood and little feathers sticking to his shirt."

"Right. Well, it's his brother that's the groom and he's the one that invited us. And everybody else, I guess."

The crowd truly was enormous. Dennis told me this would go on for the better part of the night. Weddings, he said, lasted days, with parades and preparatory baths and parties like this one, and then the ceremony.

"So tomorrow's the big day?" I asked. The groom had dismounted and hoisted someone else onto his own shoulders. "They'll do this all night?"

"Yeah, and without any help." He pointed over to a far corner where a group of young men were huddled, distant from the rest of the gathering. "Except those guys. And that's why they're by themselves. Nobody wants to have anything to do with people using alcohol.

"So tomorrow's the day, yeah, and he'll be married. In the morning his best man will come and wake him up and give him a long hot bath. Then he'll shave all of his body hair and perfume his body. And they'll go to the wedding. It's a big deal."

"What about for the women?" I asked off hand. He paused a moment.

"The women. Well, I don't know so much. It's hard to know everything that happens when you're a man and especially a foreigner because the women keep to themselves. I bet my wife knows stuff I don't know because she's a woman. She's a woman, so she can be confided in. And that makes sense. It's sort of like two communities, the men and the women.

"But the biggest thing for the woman happens the night after the wedding." He turned to me and went slowly, trying to emphasize as clearly as possible his ambivalence about the situation. "That night she and her new husband go into a room in their new house. Except that lots of new couples will live for some time with her family. So they go into a room. And the whole time they are in there, the family stands outside the door waiting. The women especially wait just outside, right at the door, and they pound on the door and yell for the groom to hurry up and get finished. Then," Dennis grinned a little but became serious again immediately, "when he's done the deed, he comes out and all the women run inside to see the bride and the sheets."

I looked at him hard. The music pumped on behind us. No one needed alcohol with that kind of energy filling the night. "They inspect her?"

"Yeah, or her sheets. It's a matter of family pride. And the next day they hang the sheets out the window to show everybody. That there was blood."

I looked at the hundreds of dark apartment windows around us. Sheets, towels, t-shirts hung on cords strung from wall to window. Pots and bricks pinned pants hems to sills, the legs flapping in infrequent breezes. The music should blow through them, I thought. Hundreds of stained white sheets hung invisibly from every dark pane of glass like curtains, screens, flags. "What if they aren't stained?"

Dennis didn't have an answer. "I don't know. I don't know. It has to happen, but I've never heard about it. But I'll bet the groom doesn't get nearly so angry as the mothers do."

After a short conversation with a few boys playing on the party's edge and some long forgotten small talk between ourselves, we walked back to our beds. Dennis and I didn't really know what we were talking about. Dennis' seriousness during the conversation portrayed perfectly his fascination with the tradition and his disdain of it. He didn't want to be a part of inspecting anyone's sheets, not his infant son's when they were wet and not his daughter's when she was married. But he had come to work with Palestinians in the organizing of the Deaf Club and of churches and to live with them in solidarity, and he couldn't see his place in the society clearly enough to justify vocalizing his displeasure with the practice. He was opposed not only to the invasion of privacy that the tradition perpetrated, but also to the restriction of individual freedom in the name of familial pride that it constituted. But he was a guest, a well-received visitor and a friend. To what effect would protesting the practice be anyway, he wondered. And the disconcerting fact lingered that the women were the main actors in the scenario.

That night I dreamed of hopelessly trying to find a suitable place to spend a honeymoon in the crowds of Gaza. The next day was a Friday, the Islamic Sabbath and the Gazan weekend, and Dennis took me down to the beach with his daughter and son. Maria danced in the sand, and Daniel began throwing our shoes at us. They bounced off my head and I collapsed gently into his lap. Encouraged, he bombed me the rest of the afternoon.

A family situated near us finished their late picnic and the children ran into the water. The skinny son shrieked in the April water and paled from the cold in his Speedos. The father stripped to his own bathing suit and ran after him, scooping him up and tossing him into the tide. Two young daughters jumped waves, shorts and t-shirts clinging to their ribs. Their mother strolled in the surf's edge, barefoot but covered completely in layers of black. Dennis noticed my gaze.

"Sometimes when it's really hot you'll see a group of women rolling around in the surf. Pushing each other, playing. They'll get completely soaked and never take off an inch of their clothes."

"She seems content," I suggested. He nodded to say, 'Who knows?'

In the following days I tried to ask Nemat about

the importance of family for Palestinians. The questions were half-formed and confused; I wasn't getting at what I wanted to ask. Directly broaching the subject of 'women' seemed too maladroit. It would be like those conversationalists who only speak to African-Americans about slavery. The attempt to understand someone dies under the weight of his or her categorization. To start dwelling on the subject of "Women in Gaza" after all the talks with Nemat seemed distracted and stereotypical. Nevertheless, I was asking under a weak guise.

I knew from the weeks I'd been in Gaza how supremely important relatives were. Religion and family were the two dominant standards of traditional Palestinian life, and almost all life in the Gaza Strip was traditional.

"Family is most important for Palestinians," she told me flatly. "Next to God and religion, family is everything. That is why we do not understand all of these stories that we hear about divorce from America. And your President. Without my mother I would just die." I chuckled at the last phrase. No matter how I tried, I couldn't fit Nemat's blatant affection into the mouth of some good friends of mine in France and the United States. It's not that they don't love their mothers. It simply would never occur to them to express their love, especially as Nemat had.

"But what about obeying? You disobey your parents by being so brazen, right?"

My teasing fell flat. "I do not disobey my mother and father! They know who I am, and they respect my ideas, and I respect what they tell me to do. Other people may say what they like about me, but I do not have to listen to them."

"I see." I had nothing to say to follow her indignation.

"People have been talking to you? What are they saying?—No. I do not want to know. That you would even listen to them—" She dropped the sentence in her anger. After a moment of distractedly shuffling papers, she looked up. I was leaning back in a chair for six-year olds and righted to four legs when she began again. "Scott, you are my friend, and you are letting these other people change your mind. You are letting them confuse you, and now it is hurting me. Do you want to do that? You have to trust me when I say this is good or this is not. You are not from here and you do not know the culture. So if you do something people will not blame you, they will say you have only made a mistake."

"Am I doing something wrong?" I asked blandly. She fumed in frustration.

"It is not wrong because you do not know that it is wrong, and it is not wrong for me because I know it should not be like this. Should it be wrong to talk to another person when you want, for a man and a woman just to talk about religion or America or whatever?"

I asked again, stoically, that she try to appreciate my angle as well. I was a guest. My behavior reflected on my hosts, the foreign humanitarian workers, Madraset Atfaluna and Gerry Shawa. If I made a mistake, everyone would excuse me. I would be a clown, slightly immoral for talking so much, but still only a harmless fool to laugh at and correct. But the correction would mean that I should be more careful and, as a guest, continuing to violate tradition could hurt the reputation of my hosts. It was not that I agreed with all of the customs of Gaza, but I could not break them all either. What good would it do? Who would care, and couldn't it do more harm than good? If I flagrantly snubbed traditions other than my own, wouldn't that strength the traditions? I was a poor accomplice, and no matter how much I desired her freedom, I couldn't be her dove.

People had begun to talk to me, pulling me aside and softly reprimanding me. "Do you see us talking to women like that?" they asked. "Better to listen than talk so much. Why not visit a different class tomorrow instead?" As I read the faces and hands that grew more imploring with the days, I rarely found any traces of jealousy or spite. From a distance, others betrayed suspicion and distrust of me as an U.S. American and a non-Muslim, and I understood their concern. But those who corrected me showed interest as pure as could be hoped in preserving my own integrity and effectiveness. "If you want to be helpful, you have to bend some," they admonished.

As their guest and colleague, I listened. I tried to walk an unspoken compromise, avoiding Nemat for half the school day by occupying myself with chores. Sometimes whole days would pass without our conversing. But the solution only aggravated the problem. Nemat felt slighted and, through her suspicions, betrayed. Our friendship seemed to have suddenly collapsed without any warning or explanation. She began to call my apartment to talk, to find out why, to mend whatever was broken. When I asked a Palestinian friend about the situation over a meal, he dropped his fork.

"She called you?" Then he bowed his head and studied a half-eaten tomato, charred at the edges. "Nemat must learn to follow our traditions." I tried to persuade her not to call again. Some nights I unplugged the phone from its jack.

The tragedy in this was the decay of our friendship. Her beginning role of guide for me at Atfaluna quickly expanded into that of teacher. I fused into her class of first-graders and practiced the flow of written Arabic and its chopped, full-throated intonation. As a student, regardless of how sincere my study was, I had glimpsed the force of creativity and care that passed from her to her pupils. They were alive because of her. When her lesson was interrupted they implored her to resume as quickly as possible. She generated in them not only the desire to learn. A real happiness had come to inhabit her place and they drew from it during the morning class hours.

I watched the way other women in the school came to her class during breaks to sit and converse in the minute pauses between Nemat's instructions. The light in Aycha was innate, but Nemat shared the same fire, and her example encouraged her admiring students. All but a handful of the men prodded her with jokes and laughed freely as they passed each other in the halls. Her openness created a natural allegiance in her colleagues towards her. But in all of her interactions she never sought to antagonize the sensibilities of others. If she disagreed with someone they surely knew it. She would not bend to their rule. But she persisted in maintaining their peace and liberty of opinion. She conceded them the pressure of tradition and did not expect that they would fully respect her choices.

She was a woman fully aware of the place of Palestinians in the world, though she'd never been beyond the border. She was a Palestinian fully aware of the role of women in her culture. Both situations were not only unjust in her mind; they were incomplete, and she had determined by a force inherent in her to finish what was undone. That force was joy. Even when work wore her thin and foreign idiots muddled her hopes, Nemat was indefatigably happy. One night in the enormous silence of my dark apartment I listened to her rail at me through the telephone receiver. Suddenly she fell into seizures of laughter without transition; the image of my wearied face enduring her rant had suddenly appeared like a vision. She couldn't block the laughter despite herself.

She had become the saint I was seeking. Without conscious intention she incarnated the hope and determined purpose vital to pushing the world into a fuller state. She had become a teacher at Atfaluna because she knew there was need, and the problem presented to her was that of deaf Palestinian children. But she was no nationalist or religious patriot. She wasn't even gearing a revolution for women under Islamic subjugation. She worked with her students, she chatted with her colleagues, she laughed with me and hounded me because her bliss led her to us and we asked for her care.

And somewhere in the middle of my vision of her goodness, Nemat had found a back door and slipped out. She was no one's saint and the only enemies facing her had put themselves into that position by virtue of their own fear.

She had become my friend. I spoke to her not as a teacher or heroine but with the respect of honesty that only friendship allows. I was unwilling to give in to her demand of trust and complicity. I valued the gift my hosts had offered too much. But if there is value in the fact, I labored to communicate to her the sincerity of my confusion.

On an evening when a more hospitable mood held sway over my emotions I was entertaining a friend from the Deaf Club. The teapot was just coming to a boil when the phone rang.

"I'll get it," my guest offered, and he picked up the receiver. "Yes, all right." He looked at me with a sober face. "It's Ahed, Nemat's brother. He's at the gate and would like to come up."

"Right," I replied. My friend's face was unreadable. "Tell him I'll be right down to let him in." I turned off the stove and sat to pull on my shoes.

I met Ahed half way down the stairwell. "Dennis was coming out and he let me in," he explained. I forced a smile and shook his hand firmly. "I am very glad to visit you tonight," he told me. I nodded my civil agreement.

Seated around the coffee table, conversation lagged. The arrival of Nemat's brother was not completely unexpected. He had passed word through Nemat many times that he still hoped to see me before the end of my stay. But I had turned down numerous occasions to visit their family at home, and Ahed's unannounced arrival seemed tinged with mischief. Nemat couldn't take no for an answer. Through her brother she had come vicariously. I felt disrespected and embarrassed. The visitor already with me had advised me many times to be wary of how liberally I interacted with Nemat, and he was a good friend of their family.

I restlessly fixed tea and scrounged for more cookies. Ahed sat stiffly in his chair and stared at the steaming cups. Talk wandered aimlessly and circled dulling themes. For the fifth time I asked the scores from the Deaf Club soccer games I'd attended the night before. Ahed nursed his tea, then asked for another cup. There was nothing to say. I was glad to busy myself with reheating the water.

Again the phone rang. My first guest answered and passed the receiver to Ahed. He spoke for a moment in clipped Arabic, then turned to me.

"Scott."

"Yes?" I called from the kitchen. The propane in the stove was waning. I couldn't get the eye to light and was nursing a finger burned from a match I hadn't extinguished soon enough.

"It's Nemat. I will have to go, that is why she is calling me. But if you would like to go with me, I could bring you back to your apartment in a few hours."

I looked at him for a moment through the counter window and answered. "No, thank you Ahed. I don't think I can come tonight. I already spoke with Nemat today and told her I would not be able to come." He repeated my words into the phone and offered it to me. Nemat and I exchanged words briefly. At work she had asked me to visit and later in the afternoon she had called. Her persistence bordered on begging, and I was put out. We scolded each other. We waited in silence for an apology. Neither gave any ground. We looked forward to seeing each other the next day.

Ahed broke the silence. "So I must go, but do you just mind if I pray first? It would only take a moment, and then I will be leaving." The request lightened my thoughts a bit. I stopped thinking about manipulation and answered with the first relaxed smile of Ahed's visit.

"Please. The bathroom's just through the bedroom, so you can wash. Take all the time you want and call if you need anything."

He bowed courteously. "No, that will be fine. All I need is some water, and perhaps a blanket. I will be very brief, but thank you."

We sat quietly, listening to the faucet run, stop, run. Water splashed in the basin. The dull knock of Ahed's knees timed his prostrations.

It only occurred to me later that I might have doubted Ahed's intentions. He could have been proving his family's piety to me in answer to some of the poorer rumors I had heard. But he had asked with the naturalness of Nemat's teasing. He wasn't trying to make a point. These were his evening prayers, and the strain tingeing his voice revealed concern that he was overstepping his bounds. He was afraid the fiasco of visiting and then inviting me might have angered me enough to cause me to throw him out.

But he had made me happy. In a simple sense, I felt honored. The feeling came not so much from knowing that he felt comfortable praying in my temporary home or from any exalted idea about religion. The act made me happy. He had simply prayed, and I was made happy. He reappeared with wet hair, sleeves pushed up, to thank me and excuse himself.

"I am happy to have been here."

"Let me walk out with you," I offered.

"No, no, I insist," he motioned to my other guest. "You should stay here. I'll be fine."

"All right."

"Perhaps we will see each other again?"

I laughed lightly. "Ahed, perhaps. I do not know."

"If God wills it," he murmured.

"Of course."

"Good evening." He gave a quick, courtly bow and pushed open the door.

"Ahed."

"Yes?" He searched my face in the darkening room.

"Tell Nemat that I am very happy that her brother prayed in my apartment. Please tell her, I have been made very happy."

He smiled easily. "I will," he promised.

The Saints

I slid two boxed pizzas into the back and ducked into the front passenger seat.

"Got it?" Dr. Fitzgerald asked and turned the keys in the ignition.

"We're ready," I said, and we pulled out into the street.

"Maybe we'll pick up some ice cream too, Donna'd like that," he said absently.

Turning back to me, he resumed our conversation. "So. The problem can be like this. For instance, I'm a member of a medical association of Christian doctors. And I get their trimesterly publication. Of course, every article dealing with abortion is ethically opposed to the practice, and I share that conviction. What doctor wants to kill? But sometimes an abortion is appropriate, to save the mother, for example.

"But then I'm at the hospital, and a girl comes in with her whole family crowding around her. She's unmarried and she's pregnant, and her family is enraged. Because the whole situation is so shameful to them. Because it's absolutely, it's absolutely opposite of what the culture expects.

"And the situation is this: the abortion is performed and no one finds out, or the family may kill the girl. Not the majority, but some families here, they would do that.

"So then what do I do? I've sworn to save life, I'm convinced it's why I'm here. And the delivery would not threaten the mother or the child. So...?

"Thank God it hasn't happened to me yet." He leaned forward in his seat as if he were sighing and turned the car down the side street to his house.

Durban, KwaZulu Natal, South Africa
4 - 31 May 1999

We together in this city—
Poor to rich, race to race,

Skin to skin, anger to anger—
We in this city together.

"I get upset when people talk about South Africa as a violent place now, South Africa degenerating and falling apart." She looked back at me quietly, her eyes returning from wandering across the wall, across the ceiling. She wouldn't look at me when we actually spoke. "Apartheid was a violent system. That's what we are still dealing with today. Like being weak from an infection, and the doctor took a long time to come."

She turned her face back toward me and stopped pulling at her purple shirt's hem. Her eyes opened wider, and she rocked slightly in her chair. Silence held between us. She waited to see what might be said next, who might say it. I understood it would be best if I spoke in turn.

"Violence was inherent in the system." My reply caught between confirmation and question, a half-statement to show that I followed her and that I would rather listen. She corrected me gently.

"Not just in the system. The system came from thoughts and feelings. We made it, and it made us." Her use of the word "we" was gracious but her expression didn't betray consciousness of this. Though she, as a Zulu, had been victimized by white South African rule, she thought in collective terms.

Outside in the adjoining office something fell, and she started with the resounding crash. Then she chuckled quietly, bending forward a little and rubbing her eyes with the palm of one raised hand. She came back to the topic but smiled despite our return to gravity. "But maybe you will see this, we will talk to you more about it. But tell me, what do you want to do here?"

"He's studying good people doing good work in developing countries. So I told him we'd come here to you instead of sticking around with me." Nise Malanga, my contact, gave a side-ways grin and stepped into our talk. "See, I come here to learn what it means to be a good person doing good work."

Nise was actually the person I had come to see. My Cape Town contact had heard of a poetess and peace activist in Durban who had used drama and poetry readings to politically educate Zulu and Xhosa people during the end of the apartheid era. She traveled throughout South Africa but especially in her native Cape province and KwaZulu-Natal, performing sketches to incite activism, to show people what they were fighting against and how to do it. In KwaZulu-Natal, some of the most important and delicate work she focused on was reunifying

African political factions that had been split through the interference of the apartheid government, especially the African National Congress (ANC) and the Inthaka Freedom Party (IFP), a Zulu nationalist group. Now she organizes reconciliation groups, bringing together South Africans of all colors and social levels to talk about grievances and resentment through poetry workshops. After welcoming me to Durban with her grand smile and a laugh, she sobered to apologize.

"I've got an Afro-Caribbean drama group from Montreal here for two weeks, and I just can't do everything with you that I want. But I did some poetry therapy once with a group that helps victims of political violence and they say you can come see if you want to work with them. I'm going to help you find something, we just have to figure out what."
I agreed. My Thailand contact's decision to surprise Phra Phongthep in Chiang Mai five months earlier had loosened any preconceived agenda tucked in my brain. If one thing didn't work out, another surely would, and I could see in her happiness that I was in good hands. We went off to find my hotel.

A few days later Nise joined me for a discussion with the coastal office directress of the KwaZulu-Natal Program for Survivors of Violence (PSV). Zandile Nhlengetwa shook my hand lightly. She spoke at a barely audible level, welcoming me, her voice gaining strength in the last syllables of her hello. I couldn't tell if her retiring manner was wariness of a snooping stranger with a funny accent or simply gentleness. Although I more than merit cautiousness, especially when applying to volunteer in a non-government organization run by ANC activists, the days proved her tranquil and trusting in me. She always spoke free of aggressiveness. Her tone made me want to be as honest and clean in expression as possible.

"I have been traveling and working with people who have given themselves in service to others," I explained. "I do that by volunteering so that I can understand the work they do, what problems they are trying to solve, what makes them want to do that work. So I want to learn from you, but I want to do anything I can to help you too. If you need typing done, I can type, or run errands, or anything." I hesitated, smiling. She waited, and I went on. "And if I will only be in the way, or if I make problems, then I don't want to be here. If I can't help here, there's somewhere else I should be. But, but I guess it is true that I want to study you." I looked down in bashfulness and then back up to find her still quiet, rocking in her chair a little, chewing on her lip. When I looked at her she looked away, then came back to meet me.

"It's very good. This project is good. We will find something for you to do. Maybe with the youth groups. Maybe you can go out with Nanty this afternoon to one of their youth meetings. He goes to a township every afternoon at about one and they have their meeting. Wait and I will ask him." She stepped out of view into the next office, asking for Nanty.

Nise and I sat for a moment. I looked at her. "She's very kind, so quiet."

"Yes." She thought on it, then continued. "Za is one of those people like a rock, so quiet and strong too. But she has lots of moss on her that makes her nice to lean on." Zandile came back into the room in time to catch the end of Nise's metaphor and started probing for the full story.

"What's this? What's this? Who do you lean on?"

They were like two kindergarteners in the way they teased each other. Nise bit her lip and shook her head to refuse telling. But with me laughing and Za so confusedly happy with the attention, beaming in her chair and consumed with wanting to know what had been said, Nise started to chortle. She tried to suppress her laughter and her cheeks inflated for a moment behind sealed lips; then her mouth puckered and she wheezed out laughing, giving way to her mirth. "You're like a rock, hard as a rock!" she said, and Za moved from giggling to all-out laughter. She laughed more quietly than she spoke; though her body lolled around in the yellow chair like a punching bag, not a sound came from her open mouth. She guffawed noiselessly.

They laughed so hard that they cried, and as their tears slowed they joked, Nise in Xhosa and Za in Zulu, until they had regained their composure. Za turned to me and teased about my third-party status. "Poor boy, sitting here listening to two crazy old women laughing in Zulu," which was enough to send Nise into a last stomach-clutching row of giggles.

As Nise calmed in her chair, Zandile reached out and patted me quickly on the forearm. "Nanty is going out this afternoon to a township, and I think you can go. He's not here right now, but some of the others say he'll be back before he leaves and you can go with him, I'm sure."

"Za?" A woman looked in through the open door.

Her thick hair was pulled back tight across her scalp.

"Uhmmm?"

"Nanty's just come in, Za."

"Oh!" she exclaimed lightly, never losing her reserve, and hopped heavily out of her chair. Before she reached the door a short man, well built in loose jeans, came over the threshold.

"Ay, Za," he murmured. His hands wandered through his jeans' pockets and he rocked on his heels, scanning the room. We caught eyes and he nodded curtly.

"Hey, Nanty. Do you think," she began, and I caught something in her words, in the tone or rhythm of the sentences. They were speaking in English for my benefit. I'd been in the office less than half an hour and had heard Zulu in the side room and between Nise and Za. But it hadn't come to my attention that English wasn't the first language of use in the offices. Here was unassuming kindness. They were illustrating that I could trust them, that nothing needed to be hidden. "Do you think someone could go out with you to the youth meeting today?"

"Yes, I think we can."

"Where are you going?"

"Ahh, we're going out to Umbumbilo this afternoon, yes." He waited to know who might join him without asking and without looking at me.

"Nanty, this is Scott, Scott—"

"Scott Neely," I stood, extending my hand. He took it, grinned, looked away from us all at the far wall, rubbed his chin.

"Hello."

"Hello."

"And this is Nanty Mbathe. He is the coordinator," she was pleased with the situation, she pulled on her shirt hem and leaned forward a little as if bowing, "of our youth program. He organizes," she rocked on her heels and laughed under the words, "our youth groups and meetings, to try to help them build some small business, to help them with their problems, like this."

"Thank you." I wanted him to understand my pleasure at being able to start so soon and my respect for whatever his work was. At that point I didn't really understand what anyone in the program did.

"Okay," he drawled, nodding to see if anything else needed to be said. By way of ending, Za added I'd go with him at one, that we would meet in the office at 12:30. Nanty went down the hall to his office, and we sat to finish talking. Nise wished me luck and excused herself to go meet the Canadian theater company. Za handed me some old newsletters to gain an idea of what the work in Survivors of Violence was like. I sat in the secretary's office to read. Nanty walked in, made a phone call, and then turned to me.

"Hey, Scott, I've got to go out to Amawoti now."

"Ama wha-what—"

The secretary laughed and didn't look up from her computer. "Amawoti. It's one of the townships out near Phoenix, KwaMashu, like that."

"Okay." I looked at him, trying to guess where his report to me was leading.

He stared my idiocy back in the face, then mocked me gently. "Yeah, so if you want to go with me now you can go, but we have to go now."

In a dark blue sedan we rose along the bypass out

of the city. A ramp took us from the midmorning traffic and over the Indian market spilling across the street, cloth and food in baskets hanging down from a long covered porch. Uncovered hills replaced the city suburbs.

Conversation was calm and intermittent. Neither pressed the other for questions. He drove and we watched rural KwaZulu-Natal spread around us.

"These out here, these are also townships?"

"Yeah, up there is one, and further up is Phoenix. Phoenix, that's an Indian township. And this one you can see—," he pointed across me to a denuded hill with unpainted cinder block buildings that looked like out-houses—"this one is a new settlement that the government built, but nobody will live there. It's for squatters, but they say they would rather live in cardboard shacks than in those houses."

"Why is that?" The personless community was lost behind another hill.

"You know, they built those houses for public housing, and some of those houses have only one room. And they have no indoor plumbing, no running water or toilets in the house."

"Why did they build them?"

"Those squatters, they need better housing now. When we come back I'll show you where some of them live. Maybe you didn't see it when we drove past. But they say that if they move in now, the government won't fix those problems. They'll just say that they already gave them houses and they are okay for houses, so they can't do more now."

I was disappointed to hear that the government, Mandela's federal administration or Durban's city managers, would fall so short of excellence. "But if the squatters wait, they might get something better."

"That's what they think, yes. They speak up and wait." His tone betrayed approval of their action. His work, as I would learn, involved organizing communities to care for their own needs. From his point of view the squatters had undertaken exactly what they needed to do in order to achieve a better life. Nanty knew how difficult it is to get people to work cooperatively, and he admired their solidarity.

Weeks later another employee of Survivors of Violence would vent frustration regarding a subject similar to that of government housing. One day his sociology and public policy professor was lecturing, he said, and started to talk about how poor the people in a certain township were. He talked about the misery of their situation, about how it was unequaled in South Africa, these people living in tiny wooden houses without proper water and sanitation. "It is because they are so poor," the professor said. "We must find some way to battle unemployment to help these people find work."

The employee looked at me. "That professor," he fumed, "he's trying to teach us how to help our country, and he doesn't even know what all the problems are. Those people in that settlement have jobs. They are poor but not like the people out in KwaMashu or Pineville. They stay up there because they think they will be able to build better homes when they have more money. They stay there instead of going to government housing because they don't want to lose their land and have to buy more later, and at a higher price. They're smart, saving their money and not buying the next shiny thing that comes along. So that professor," he lowered his voice and looked at me, trying to make sure I understood so that I could guard myself against the same error, "just looked at the way people were living and used a national problem formula to explain their situation. He never talked to them to find out the truth. He doesn't know what's really happening."

Nanty and I drove out to Amawoti that morning to visit members of a youth group at their homes. They had been invited to participate in an Outward Bound weekend, and he needed to check with a few people who hadn't confirmed their spot for the program. As we turned off the highway and started out to the first house down a baked clay road, he started to explain the weekend leadership program.

"They will go and spend the time hiking for a long while, and then they will even spend a day solo, all alone. It's scary for an African kid from the townships." He laughed a little to himself, imagining the faces of some of his colleagues alone and jitterish out in the bush.

The idea surprised me. South African townships bear many of the same characteristics as Native American reservations in the United States. Purposefully constructed without any economic institutions of their own, the absence of industry or business pulled fathers from their families in the townships to the cities. The absence of schools left children without education or, when schooling was possible, took them from their homes. The townships are outside of the main cities, in rural areas expanding out into the countryside. As with traditional Cherokee or

Lakota, I had assumed that the Zulu would express a respect and a love of unadulterated nature that encouraged a desire to be in it. The idea that fear of the wilderness would take a people once vitally allied with the natural world and living so much more closely to it than those of us in cities like Durban hadn't occurred to me.

Nanty offered an explanation. "See, back during apartheid, these people would have to run out into the bush to hide from the police. Not that they had necessarily done anything wrong, but the police terrorized us. And they'd stay out all night, sometimes for many days. Especially these people our age, they would be fighting against the police, fighting to end apartheid, and have to run from their homes to hide in the hills. So they don't see it as beautiful and peaceful so much as a place of fear. They could have been hiding, but then they could have been found too."

"So this Outward Bound program is more than just team-building for the youth groups."

"Yeah, so that's also why we have to come out here today to make sure they will come. Because they might not come, you see."

That morning we drove through Amawoti. We picked up Thanbi, a young member of the youth group, and she guided us to the homes of people still unconfirmed for the trip. She wore flip-flops and a pink leotard with a red cloth wrapped about her waist like a sarong. Guardedly kind, she kept her eyes turned from us, looking out the window. With her right arm propped against the door she would run her fingers lightly over the rubber window lining.

Nanty teased her in Zulu and she laughed, looked further out the window, out past the township.

"Are you ready?" I asked.

"Yes," she said as slowly as a yawn, and laughed again. Nanty kept mumbling, pricking her with jokes in a low voice. "I am ready." Then she dropped her hand and leaned forward. "You are going too?"

"No," I said. "I'll be in Chile by then."

"Chile." She leaned back and returned to gazing beyond us. "What do you think of the program?" she asked, lingering over the drop of each word.

"I think it will be strong for you all," I said. Nanty pumped his arm once to mock both Thanbi and me, and we all sighed out laughter.

Some back roads were too steep or rutted to pass in a car, and Thanbi and I would wait while Nanty trudged off to check with a family on an opposite hill. It was a quiet morning. Thanbi avoided unnecessary conversation and always evaded eye contact. I watched around me.

The hill we stood on folded into another like the muscles in a palm, as if we stood at the heel of a green hand. The landscape lay open before us, balanced by a clean sky as expansive as the country. The essential memory marked in my mind from that first trip to the townships with Nanty is the light on those hills.

Out in the townships some hillsides hold no grass or trees. Roads have worn in ruts, and rain has carried off the green. From where I stood in Amawoti I could see little houses peppering the shallow valleys. They were simple, usually only a few rooms large at most, sometimes constructed of lumber or cinderblock, some frailer and made of scrap metal, tar paper, and weathered wooden slats. Out in some districts of KwaMashu mud huts, circular and tall, outnumber other kinds of housing. Everywhere one sees reminders of the fight to stay above water, to keep providing for family and to maintain respectability. The drive from downtown Durban's glass skyscrapers to the township neighborhoods draws a line between two related and inseparable realities. One family's poverty and dissolution built another's urbane home. But the same South African light passes over both houses, and it carried the landscape through the drive.

The light's fluidity and clarity is like water. I visited a close friend in Cape Town when I first arrived in the country. After hiking up Table Mountain I looked over the coastal city. The light spread from the South Atlantic across the bay, through the Cape Flats and Rondebosch. It illuminated everything, as if the city was an extension of the ocean.

The afternoon after our visit to Amawoti, Nanty and I drove to Mbumbulu, another township on the other side of Durban, for a regular youth meeting. In a break in the discussion, I stepped out of the old, weatherbeaten Anglican Church to be alone. Grass stood up to my waist, and the same green hills rolled into blue under my feet. The same light, now softer with afternoon shadows, swam over the land.

The meeting had convened with a prayer. Zulu is an unaggressive language, forgiving in its hesitancy and low tone. A volunteer from Survivors of Violence had met us at the meeting and planned to brief me in English on the important points, but he allowed the prayer to pass. Still, the rhythm of the Lord's Prayer is as familiar as a mass in Hindi. We sat back down and the discussion took its course.

On the drive out, I had asked Nanty to explain the purpose of the youth groups. I understood the basic work of the Program for Survivors of Violence. Started in 1994, it was essentially a mental health organization for victims of political violence. Counseling and personal development programming was offered to anyone in need regardless of political affiliation or personal history, although the main benefactors of the work were residents of the black townships. The group especially wanted to heal old wounds between the two main political organizations supporting the cause of black Africans, the ANC and the IFP. These two groups had a long history of divisiveness and intraracial violence that still erupts in the townships even after the end of the apartheid era. The hope was that by healing individuals, the native African community in KwaZulu-Natal would also begin to be healed. That reunification of the broken community would strengthen their cause in the struggle against racial discrimination and apartheid-era terror.

But after two years the PSV group began to see that they could no longer simply help people with their emotional trauma. The environment in which people in the townships lived was terribly underdeveloped and had been deliberately designed to be violent. The lack of schools and hospitals, the necessity of leaving one's family in order to find employment, and the isolation from city centers—all aspects of township life—were means by which the apartheid government eroded family and communitarian cohesiveness among black Africans. The townships were designed to make their inhabitants economically, morally, and thus politically impotent. The PSV group understood that they had to help people deal with their total environment, not just with their nerves. Their programming grew to include economic development projects in the townships as well as community leader discussion forums. The youth groups evolved out of this shift in focus.

A youth group is formed when a PSV coordinator asks a community leader for the names of people, aged 15 to 35, who have suffered some traumatic incident. The number of people to whom this pertains is uncountable. One coordinator, Dumasani, explained to me that his generation had become the freedom fighters against apartheid in the 1980s. They gave up the opportunity to go to school in order to strike against the unjust conditions of non-white facilities. They gave up their childhood in order to fight against South African police. They were the heroes of the new, fully inclusive South African democracy. Adults told me that they had been unable to defeat the apartheid system, and when their children began to act, they stepped out of the way and offered support. The youth won the battle against injustice.

But today, Dumasani explained, these heroes are seen as the culprits in the problems of society. They didn't go to school and so they can't get a job. They must rely on their younger siblings for support, which is shameful in the view of traditional values. In Zulu thought, for example, the elder siblings should provide for the younger. Some turn to drug dealing or banditry because they see no other way to make a living. Others turn to sex for comfort against their isolation, which leads to population overgrowth, increased teen pregnancy, and the spread of HIV. Combined with all of this, Zulu children are not expected to speak with their parents beyond formal conversations and obedient replies. No space for sharing hurt and loneliness exists. The heroes, he summarized, are isolated from the society they saved. Today they are seen as South Africa's weight to bear, its failed hope for the future, the "proof" of racist theories of superiority. One can read a lie into any situation if one is willing enough to ignore the cause.

The youth groups are an attempt to bring people back together. They originate as meetings in which members can begin to share their feelings, expressing their hurt and frustration. Friendships develop quickly out of these encounters, and some groups take all of their meals together, the members spending as much time with one another as possible. At a lull in the Mbumbulu afternoon meeting, one man leaned over to me and whispered, "I knew so many people before. I have always known so many people. But before this, I never had any friends."

Once the individual's isolation gives way to the formation of a real community, the PSV coordinator begins to encourage the development of an economic plan. The group conceives of some small-scale business venture—roadside stands vending refreshments to truckers, t-shirt companies, chicken farms—that it can undertake together and maintain until every member of the group has found some other, more stable employment. Many of the groups continue to meet on their own, without the guidance of a PSV coordinator, long after the business is dissolved.

Even only a few weeks after its inception, the new Mbumbulu group was already trying to conceive a business project. The meeting stumbled along under the direction of that week's moderator with Nanty interrupting from time to time to offer advice on a better way to pose a question or the importance of everybody speaking what they thought. "You have to cooperate," he said, "and that means saying what you think and then trying to combine everyone's ideas as much as possible. You have to start by sharing and talking."

I leaned back against one of the thin ashen beams, shaved white and cracking, that held up the tin roof. Aside from the occasional sentence from the interpreter, I couldn't follow the content of the discussion. But the feeling I got was that they were trying. The three women in the group had come in late and sat alone in a shadowed corner of the room. For a long time they said nothing, but after a few interruptions by Nanty encouraging everyone to participate, they began to question the wisdom of raising and selling chickens. "If everyone doesn't help care for them, all the money we give to the project could be lost. We would be in more difficulty than when we started. Now," said one, looking up from the spot she had fixed on the cement, "how can we be sure we'll all help?"

"Well, we have to trust each other…," the moderator ventured.

"And can you trust me?" she responded. "Or can I trust you?" A loud laugh shot from the back of the room. No one had mentioned the human factor in the project proposals, and she had assumed the role of devil's advocate. "I mean, we are friends now, and we live near each other. But if I am tired, how can you know that I will still go and do my part of the work?"

Almost everyone in the group tried to contribute in one fashion or another that afternoon. The meeting had its bumps—votes had to be recounted, volunteers to help with the organization and leadership of the following meeting had to be pulled from the reticent congregation. But they were doing it, feeling their way along, questioning and so encouraging each other. After the formal meeting broke, people stayed after to enjoy bologna and mayonnaise sandwiches. Conversation picked up as the group relaxed, and a comfortable murmur of talk and teasing filled the chilly sanctuary. I poured a cup of neon green cream soda for the moderator.

"Sir, what did you think?" he asked me like a student turning in a final exam.

"Don't call me 'Sir'," I laughed back at him. "You're already older than me. I think it went well, no? Already you are looking for a project."

"Yes, yes. We are trying hard. And it feels good to have some kind of work like this again, especially where we are the ones making it."

As we pulled away from the township onto the main highway, a gaggle of kids walked in front of us. Two little girls, maybe twelve years old at the most, pushed wheelbarrows full of plastic water jugs. Boxy and precariously stacked, the containers wobbled over the pockmarked street, pouting and spitting water. The children chased each other and sang by us. We pulled into the road.

Nanty came out of his musing silence and popped an unexpected question. "Do you have these 'car-jackings' back in the U.S.?"

"Yes, not so much where I live, but in the bigger cities. They say that there are some places where a person shouldn't drive at night, and some places where a person shouldn't go anytime. Especially because of wealth and race—like there are parts of Washington, DC, into which I have been told I shouldn't go because I am white and middle-class. It is just asking for trouble."

"We have places like that too," he said, then smiled and continued. "Like some parts of Mbumbulu. So go with us next time too, and not just on your own." He laughed at his own joke and came back to his first question. "No, I'm asking because we are starting to have a lot of problems with these car-hijackings. And it doesn't matter what's your race, whether you are black or Indian or white. Because I think they do it for the money, see, and so they don't care what color you are. They just want the car because they think they'll make some money off it." I thought back to Gaza and to Dennis's daughter, Maria. We used to sit in the back while he drove, trying to pick out the cars stolen in Israel and resold in Palestinian territory by the coloring of the license plate lettering.

The problem of crime has South Africa by the throat, although the government under the new president Mbeki is seeking to crack down on its main cause—unemployment. Although the new, full de-mocracy has universalized the right to equal schooling and has legally ended job discrimination, the legacy of apartheid still impedes people from living in an equal and socially just society. A Zulu may have the right to work anywhere now, but because she was denied an education equal to the one enjoyed by her fellow citizen of English ancestry she does not have the qualifications necessary for the same high level employment. Though law no longer holds her in the lowest social position, the historical effect of apartheid keeps her there.

"Who would feel loyalty to anyone else if they had to live like that?" Dumasani asked me. "So they steal and rob from anyone."

The consequence is fear. On a slow day in the Survivors of Violence office I went to the neighboring suite to speak with Annsilla, a student of Tamil descent who researches human rights law and violations for PSV and Oxfam International. I wanted to borrow the first volumes of the South African Truth and Reconciliation Committee Report, but after eyeing the thickness of only one of the tomes, we started talking instead.

For over two hours Annsilla told me stories of crime. Random acts of burglary or violence; race-hate crime of black on white, white on black, black on black, and Indian caught everywhere in between; urban myths—she went through reams of memory to try to tell me just how afraid some people were in South Africa. I talked about my surprise when Nanty had mentioned the car-jackings despite what I had read in newspapers.

"And that's the thing, though. These aren't just stories. The newspapers are reporting these things, so we know that they are really happening. A month ago," she leaned forward, "a man was walking through the mall and he was stabbed with a needle. He had to go to the hospital because they were afraid it might be infected with HIV. I don't know what they did to test him or to treat it, but you see, there may be people walking around infecting others just because they are angry, maybe because they are sick or because of old racism problems."

"And think about what it must be like for a woman. I tell you not to be out after dark, and so does Za. And how do you think we feel, even more? But you also look like you could be Afrikaans or Anglo South African. No one can know until they talk to you. So you are kind of an open target, especially because you aren't from here and you don't know what to look for."

"What *do* you look for?" My palms sweated handprints on the book cover.

She thought, then laughed. "I don't know. You just are careful somehow and hope for the best, I guess. I try to always walk with a friend. Don't look people in the eyes. But you can't spend your whole life worried about a bomb in your car, can you?"

"No."

That afternoon I rode six flights down the elevator and watched the doors slide open to the world of downtown Durban at five in the afternoon. The sidewalks were already full. The opening of the doors was like a gun going off at the start of a half-mile race to my hotel. Everything Annsilla told me had been rumbling around in my head since lunch, and now it began to roar. All I could think about was the possibility of getting into trouble. The thought of being pricked by an infected needle just because I was a

scrawny white kid stuck in my mind like a dart. I
pulled my shirtsleeves all the way down and gripped
them with my fingers, trying to cover every inch of
exposed skin. I buttoned my collar all the way to the
last button and gagged for breath. I started to walk.

At the door I paused and looked at the city's body
pressing by. I have never been to New York City, but at
that moment I imagined it as a spacious and peaceful
manor compared to this rushing glut of pedestrians.
I sucked in one breath and resolved to go, then
breathed again. This time...but no, I still stood in
the same spot. Behind me the concierge laughed at
something and I swore quietly at his ridicule of me.
I plunged into the crowd.

Durban winters are milder than those in South
Carolina, but they are not summer either. My armpits
itched from sudden, hyper sweating. The crowd
moved over me and I walked as close to a run as I
could, trying not to look anyone in the eye, avoiding
every possible gaze, and consequently almost top-
pling everyone around me with my reckless gait.
"Don't touch anybody"—the thought pounded
through my brain, and I slipped past people, making
myself as narrow and inconspicuous as possible,
sliding through gaps and ducking through passage-
ways. If anyone had stopped to look up, a traffic jam
would likely have occurred for the laughter at my
show.

I jumped up the steps to my hotel and went
straight to my room. Collapsing on the bed I breathed
into the pillow and eventually undid my top shirt
button. "Fear is only a mental formation, a thought to
be extinguished by understanding it," I quoted, trying

to find solace in half-baked Buddhist convictions. I could feel a thousand needles pricking my forearms.

Through the hotel walls televisions cheered cricketers. An elderly person laughed into her phone. The whole world was normal and I was exhausted. Thirteen hours later I woke up, very hungry and resolved to walk to work.

The morning sun lightened the weight of skyscrapers. Their glass shells reflected the sky's bright blue. Without incident and with confidence building again, I stepped into the elevator and rode six floors up to the Survivors of Violence office. Za greeted me with her sweet maternity.

"Do you care for some tea?" she asked with overstated politeness. With Za, everything was worth mockery. We sat over our cups for a while. I coughed from the freedom the steam brought to a cold I'd been nurturing a few days.

"Listen to you," the secretary giggled. I blew my nose.

"Scott," Za said with some authority. "I've got just the thing for your cold. We should help it before it gets out of hand." She reached in her purse and pulled out two lemons wrapped in a produce-section bag. "When my children are sick, I give them a lemon to eat."

"Eat a lemon?" I looked at her to see if this was another joke. Nanty came into the office and went back out laughing, having understood immediately what was going on.

"Yes, we do it all the time when we are sick."

"Listen, I have always heard that citrus fruits are good for colds because of vitamin C. And I have been eating oranges and drinking juice. But I don't think a lemon—"

"No, it's good, it will help," she urged. The whole office was watching now, waiting to see if I would trust Za.

"I just peel it and eat it?"

"Yes."

"The whole thing?"

"Right, all of it. It's good. Good for the chest." She patted her chest.

I started to peel the first fruit and when finished broke it in halves along its natural seam.

"Are you sure?" I asked.

"Eat it," she nudged.

After I swallowed the first bite, the clogging contents of my lungs no longer impeded my ability to breathe. Through all of the riotous laughter that my soured face caused, I saw red come up in Za's cheeks. I rushed sputtering to the bathroom to deal with the lemon's effects.

When I came back, still crying from the acid and bitterness, everyone was laughing. "Did you eat it all?" Za asked.

"It's all gone," I choked out, not reporting the half I'd flushed down the toilet. "God save me, Za, why did you give that to me?"

"But you're doing better now," she laughed. "Here, you take this one and I'll bring you two more tomorrow."

"No, that's all right, I'll be sure to buy some, you don't worry with it. It's my cold anyway." She looked doubtfully at me.

"You know, when my children are sick —"

"You do this to your children?!" I exclaimed. The room went into another seizure of laughter.

"Yes, yes. And they like it. We all do it, it makes us better just like that." She tossed the second lemon and snatched it from the air. "And we put cayenne pepper on it too, and sometimes if there are no lemons, we use chilies instead."

"Thank you for sparing me," I bowed.

"Well, listen. Listen now. We are family. When you have some problem, we want to help you with it." She chuckled out of the room.

The unity with which the office of Survivors of Violence worked testified to the ideal of community building for which they strove. Granted, some days could seem chaotic, the team disjointed, individuals out and unable to be reached. But on the whole, the group at PSV functioned magnificently, cohesively, cooperatively. In the end, I suppose that the explanation for their success is simple. They lived what they taught because it worked so effectively.

I found beautiful the ease with which they reconciled the often opposed virtues of community and efficiency. Work was done and done well. Perhaps their focus helped the group remain together, progressing with little deterrence from their goals. They concentrated on healing.

When working with individuals, the counselor would route that person to a support group. Along with the youth gatherings in the townships, peer counseling and small topic-discussion forums served to connect a single person to others dealing with similar issues. They thus worked to help others like themselves as a part of their becoming whole.

Groups also functioned so as not to lose the individual in their mechanization and progress toward a given end. In the youth meetings, a different member presides over the gathering every week. After the first few meetings, the PSV employees and volunteers who attended the youth groups did little more than encourage members that had not spoken to engage in the discussion. They constantly asserted the importance of voicing concern and outright dissent in a democracy. Women especially were urged to participate more, and they encouraged each other to speak the advice that they usually preferred to whisper only to their girlfriends.

Through such constant attention to communicating well and keeping everyone connected to the collective work, the program for Survivors of Violence and its many branch groups shared a familial feeling. Within the community and especially among employees, people felt relaxed. Happiness welcomed everyone, daily, into the offices—happiness born of successful, morally and politically progressive work, and of friendship, the ultimate good produced by communal commitment.

Thus when Za humorously scolded me for trying to deal with my sickness alone, pulling everyone in the office suite in to see me gag on lemons, she showed me that I had a place. I brought happiness to them. I helped them in my own meager way. Perhaps even just my continued interest in the work, a curiosity that brought me back everyday, sufficiently immersed me in the life of PSV to make me a part. When she told me that I was family, she meant it.

In the early afternoon on a day late in my stay, I came back into the PSV office suite with a handful of boxes filled with steaming pastries. Hungry and unable to find anything other than packets of tea and a half-empty two liter bottle of neon green cream soda in the office's cabinets, I'd stepped down six floors and half a block to pick up some lunch at the corner pastry shop. The stand had been busy and the wait long. My hunger grew from the mixture of my impatience and the smell of meats and sugar baking under bread. By the time my turn had come to order I asked for over a dozen, knowing that what my ravenous appetite couldn't consume, others in the office would polish off.

The aroma of hot bread wafting down the corridor drew a fair crowd into the main office. Half the employees hadn't taken lunch off, and before long we had a regular Sunday school social forming around the secretary's desk. A butter knife surfaced and managed to double the number of servings. Someone went out with a mouthful to fix tea, and the cream soda, like oil in the temple lamp at Hanukkah, circled without ever running dry.

After only two halves I was satisfied, thankful for so many other mouths to protect me from gluttony and waste. Za lounged easily against the far counter, popping another pastry in her mouth. Chewing, she stared for a while out the large window overlooking the city and, further out, Durban's industrial bay. She finished eating, paused for a moment's reflection, then turned to me.

"Scott," she said, surprised to find me already looking at her.

"Sorry I didn't do a better job cooking lunch," I toyed apologetically.

She laughed lightly and said, "I have a favor to ask of you."

"Okay."

"I've started a youth group," she began, saying each word slowly as if working the chicken from the meal out of her teeth. "At my church. And next week they will meet with other youth groups from other churches."

"It sounds good Za. You're the leader?" I had always been skeptical of youth groups, of their overly friendly directors and lightweight spirituality. But anything in Za's hands would be noble.

"Yes, but I'm worried...," she continued.

"What of?" I asked to encourage her.

She came to the point quickly. "Well, I would like your help. Because this youth group is only of Zulu and Xhosa children, I mean teenagers. And next week the gathering will have all kinds of people, all the races in South Africa. And some of the children in my group have never had a conversation with a white person before, because they come from out in the townships, some of them. So I am worried about what they will do, or about how they will be afraid and not do anything, you see?"

I nodded that I did. She explained that she wanted me to plan a unity workshop for that coming Saturday evening. As Seventh Day Adventists, their Sabbath would end at six.

"This is their first meeting, and they want to have it out on the beach. So I'll come by your hostel around 4:30 and we'll drive down to the coast. And then you can lead us into unity," she ended grandly, bowing a little, sarcastically. I bowed back.

We discussed the meeting's organization for a short time. Those still around to finish off the last pastries brainstormed possible exercises with us. As it turned out, though divided by the Atlantic, the PSV staff had participated more than once in group initiatives exactly like some of which I had been a part. Set as a game, teams are presented with challenges— untying a human knot formed by their own arms or catching each other in a trust fall, for example—that force the group to work as one.

Za thought a ropes course, even without the ropes, would meet the needs she saw in her youth. The games would help the group relax and enjoy being together while helping them teach themselves about cooperation and trust. We sat in the office, still drinking the same inexhaustible cream soda, trying to remember how the activities worked.

The following Saturday Za arrived, her son at the wheel of their station wagon. He wore a fresh white shirt with dark slacks and a black tie.

"Welcome, Brother Scott," he said, getting out of the car to open the back door for me. As I slid in Za turned in the front passenger seat and spoke to me. She was excited about the evening and a bit nervous.

"They are all already out there," she said, raising her eyebrows a little in anticipation. Her eyes questioned if I was ready.

"I hope they'll enjoy it, I hope we'll learn what you want us to see," I replied.

"They will, don't worry. This will be perfect," she said, and she turned back to give her son directions in Zulu.

A half hour later we pulled into an empty lot surrounded by hedges with thick shiny leaves. Sand had washed them along the edge of the black pavement. As I climbed out of the car I could see the sky over Durban, dark already with the night and orange where the main city stood. Wind rattled the hedge branches.

As we made our way along a sandy path, the wind gained strength, a long continuous heaving. We walked behind a high dune for about a hundred yards, Za between her son, who led us, and myself.

The path meandered, and at low points in the crest of the dune, or where the path turned as if to ascend and look out over the sea, I heard something, like a second wind low and moving underneath the breeze. For some minutes we continued walking until Za's son stepped off the path and trudged quickly up the steep sandy side.

In turning the undercurrent of sound rose again to meet us, and as we mounted the dune I saw its source. The moment before my head came over the ridge it clarified into a chorus divided neatly into two parts, female voices carrying the song and male voices harmonizing, swimming beneath the melody.

Jerusalem-a, Jerusalem-a, the song's one lyric came to us. I saw a half circle of forty or more teenagers swaying to the music. When the women sang *Jerusalem* their line moved counter-clockwise a few steps. On the *-a* that ended the word the curve hesitated, dipped, and as the men echoed *Jerusalem-a* the same movement swayed clockwise.

We walked into the middle of their group, the

wind strong now, unhindered and coming off the long dark water, our clothes pulling like flags tight against our bodies. White dresses clung to thin calves; ties flapped undisciplined and sleeves pushed past the elbow unrolled themselves. Everyone was smiling and no one would look at us, in the way we avoid eye contact with the very person we want to honor at a ceremony.

The forty voices sang. Za stood beside me and joined in the melody, putting her hands against her thick sides. I stood there unable to do much of anything, completely taken with the moment's strength.

As they sang, on and on, the circle slowly closed. Always moving a few steps to the right, then a few to the left, the ends met and the space between people lessened. The circle cinched tighter around us, continuing in rhythm with the song, until it collapsed and we formed a whole of bodies against bodies. Still they moved and sang. Skin rolled against skin like easy gears turning, on until the song gradually faded.

We did the group initiatives that night and enjoyed them thoroughly. After each game we talked about teamwork, communication, cooperation, always returning to the question of how the next week's interracial youth meeting might go and how they could lead in building community.

But my program only served as a summary of their own teaching. We had gathered to talk about unity, and they had created it. I can find no better metaphor for my time in South Africa with Zandile and those who worked in the townships and at PSV. The welcome given to me by the youth group that evening embraced a stranger into the fold. I labored alongside many saints that month—Zandile, whose maternal care and undaunted activism organized the program's work; Vusi, who welcomed me into his apartment when I needed a place to stay; Nanty and Dumasani, who led the formative township groups and guided the maturing ones; Kimberly, who welcomed me, cared for me, listened to me, and incarnated for me all things strong and redeemed. But in its unified strength and in its loving reception of me as family, finally, it was the community of the Program for Survivors of Violence that stood as an example of the life committed to doing what must be done.

The Saints

I received an e-mail just before leaving Thailand from the scholarship's anonymous donor.

"Do me a selfish favor," he wrote to play down his generosity. "Take some poor family out to a restaurant for Thanksgiving, for me. Use the back-up American Express card I gave you. Spend around U.S. $100."

My excitement at the task soon began to become frustration. Because of sickness or vows, no one at the hospice could eat as rich a meal as he wanted me to give. And I could not simply walk up to a person in the street, explain that I wanted to feed a poor family a sumptuous meal, and ask if she might not happen to be a member of a willing one. I had to make certain, as the custodian of the donor's selflessness, that the chosen family would understand the meal as a gift. I feared insulting those meant to be honored.

As I traveled, I searched. Weeks passed, then

months. Thanksgiving became Christmas and finally Easter, and my exasperation grew with time. In Israel I received another message encouraging me to treat another family with another U.S. $100.

But when I arrived at PSV, the situation clarified. Zandile, with her care and friendship, had made herself my mother of the Southern Hemisphere. This was no small undertaking for her. Left a single mother of three when her husband died, she also cared for the three children of her sister, who was working in England. Though not desperately poor—she could afford a small apartment in Durban instead of living in the townships—restaurants did not usually fit into her family's budget.

I approached her with some hesitation one day. "Za?"

"Yes?" She turned to me, still half-attentive to a letter she was reading.

"Za, I have a favor to ask of you…" I paused, then explained the situation. "Your whole family, anyone you want to invite. And you can choose the restaurant."

She beamed at me and said in her soft accents, "Scott, that would be brilliant. That would be brilliant."

I continued to try to explain my concern in asking, muddling respect with clumsy words. "I mean, I don't want to offend you. I was worried, but I wanted to ask you—"

"Scott," she said firmly, stopping me. "That would be brilliant."

Her children chose the Hilton Hotel, a place where

I also had never eaten. We stepped into the elevator to go the half floor up to the restaurant.

"Oh!" her youngest charge, an eight year old, exclaimed. The walls of the elevator were covered in shiny, silver-tinted metal and mirrors. "Do you have your camera?"

"Yes," I answered, laughing with the others.

"Then take a picture," he begged. "Cause this is what heaven is going to be like!"

Santiago de Chile

1 – 30 June 1999

That city of bodies,
That graveyard we built—

They will stand up,
They will build again
better than before.

For the final full month of my trip I had planned
to work with an international environmental organization dealing with the preservation of the Peruvian
Amazon and its peoples. But at the last minute those
plans fell through. A series of e-mails with the dean
of foreign studies at Wofford filled the space with a
possible stay in Santiago, the capitol of Chile. The
director of a study abroad program there suggested
that I might find the saint I was seeking through a
large social service organization, the Fundación Cristo
Vive (The Christ Lives Foundation). Operating in one
of the large *poblacíons*, or slum areas, of Santiago,
the foundation offered technical training in a variety
of vocations, such as carpentry and masonry. It also
offered a nursery for children whose parents were
either working or neglectful, a day care center for

severely handicapped adults, and spiritual growth programs for teenagers. Many foreigners, whether students or travelers in Chile, volunteered time there regardless of language ability, and the study abroad director assured me there would be no lack of work with which I could help.

Furthermore, she offered me the option of staying with a Chilean host family the way other foreign students often do. The questions of where I would reside and for how long posed themselves with every new venue throughout my trip. Though sometimes my hosts never thought twice about how to arrange the logistics of my visit, assuming without question that I would board with them or in the building out of which we worked, other situations had less obvious solutions, as my time in Jerusalem proved. The chance to stay in a Chilean household excited me. I would come to know more than one segment of Santiago and its population, and I hoped that the degree of separation that I would have between rest and work would afford me a space for reflection on what I was experiencing.

One morning about a week into my stay I awoke early, groggy as the city's winter smog clouding my room window, and crawled from under the mound of blankets I'd piled above me during the course of the night. Stumbling as quietly as possible down the hallway, I paused at my host parents' bedroom door. Through the crack I could only see the wall opposite their bed, the television and record player stationed low against it. The far window showed skyscrapers pink with morning and dry brown mountains just beyond. I stifled my breath to hear if they were still asleep. She rustled restlessly, but they were still in bed. Satisfied I hadn't yet disturbed them, I slipped into the bathroom.

But as I dried myself after showering, I heard water running in the pipes through the wall into the kitchen. Aside from the enticing option of taking a drip shower on a winter morning, muffling the racket of bathing is impossible. Under the mild weight of guilt at being the household alarm clock every morning I dressed and walked into the small dining room.

A basket of biscuits lay on the table already, covered by a green napkin. With her hair pulled back by a bandana and her face moist with lotion, my host mother, Carmen, turned circles in the kitchen. Despite the complete coordination of her mind and hands, she always seemed nervous to me in that thin room. Matching the adjacent corridor in length and width, filled with counters and a stove, the space only allowed her to bounce from one pot to another. Its size restricted her from going in one direction long enough to move gracefully. Above almost all other dreams she wished to expand the apartment with a larger cooking area, one with a long window that opened out past the city to the encircling mountains.

She noticed me as I pulled out the chair at my usual place and began to sit.

"Chocolate or coffee today, Scott?" she called to me.

"Chocolate please, with—"

"Milk," she completed my sentence as a mumbled thought to herself, sighing the word in mild amusement at the predictability of my taste. The first drops of milk sizzled in a pot.

"Good morning, Carmen," I said with light direct-ness as she placed jam and cheese on the table at my left hand.

"Good morning," she whispered. An absence in her voice brought my eyes up to look at her. Just as she turned away from me I glimpsed a tear caught in the bag under her eye. She was already back in the kitchen before I could get my words out.

"Carmen," I said. "Are you all right?"

"What, Scott?" She seemed not to have heard my question, or to have heard it and replied with false casualness. I watched intently as she looked every-where for the platter of sliced ham that lay beside her hand on the counter. As she came back to the table I repeated my question, measured and deliberate.

"Carmen," I said. "Is everything all right?"

She placed the ham in front of her on the table and stared softly at the wall. It seemed as if she had somehow stopped all motion around and within her for a moment, and that she was considering whether of not she might cry a little. Her hands rested gently on the back of a chair. Then she drew it out and sat down, placing her elbows on the table and slumping to rest the full weight of her head in her hands. As she bent to cover her eyes she glanced at me and began to weep quietly. I handed her a paper napkin and watched.

She sat up and smiled weakly. "Excuse me, excuse me," she gestured with her hand, waving it vaguely in front of her face.

"It's all right," I said. "Is there anything I can do?"

The chair creaked a little as she relaxed back into it. She wiped her eyes and nose a few times, looked down at the wadded napkin, set it on the table beside the ham, and began talking.

"Last night, or early this morning, I woke up. And I realized that Santiago was not in the bed beside me." Her husband, Santiago, had suffered a stroke a year earlier and had suffered almost complete paralysis down the right side of his body. That he could barely walk caused Carmen even more distress when she found him no longer in bed.

"So I got up," she continued. "And as I was standing from the bed I saw a light on across the hall, coming from under the closet door. So I called once, 'Santiago,' and then I walked to the door across the hall, and I called his name again and I opened it. And he was standing there, with his back to the door and to me, facing the wall, with his head bent down.

"I said again, 'Santiago?'" She looked at me with wide, lonely eyes, saucers of sleeplessness. "And when I placed my hand on his back, he jumped. I asked him what he was doing there but he wouldn't tell me, he said, 'Nothing,' and he was very upset. He said we should just go back to bed. So I turned to walk out. Then I heard something fall to the floor, and I bent down to pick it up.

"Down in the waistband of his sweatpants he had put a packet of his pills. His epilepsy pills. I picked them up from where they had fallen. I asked him why, what was he doing. But he did not answer, he said he didn't know what they were doing there and that we should just go back to bed. So we did, and I have not slept all night."

She pushed the little plate of ham towards me. She tried to stabilize herself with every movement, to push past fear, but she could not. Along with Santiago's stroke had come mild epileptic seizures and for months he had been on a preventative medication that acted as a heavy sleep inducer. It made him sleep throughout the night and left him deeply lethargic until almost noon of the next day. Taken again at about six in the evening, he was left with less than seven fully conscious hours in a day. That time gave him the chance to do little but feel impotent and spent. He was constantly depressed, and his virility showed itself only in flaring rages when he would insist, like a baby, that he not be made to take his medicine anymore.

His depression filled Carmen too. She worked selling clothes and baked goods, stretching money to make ends meet, devoting all the time she could to helping him with his speech therapy.

But despite her devotion, something uncommunicated stood between them. What had left her so crushed on that morning was not that Santiago might have been trying to commit suicide, though the thought terrified her. Possibly he was hiding his pills so that he wouldn't have to take them anymore, making his actions a valiant lunge at a life more alive. The real frustration lay in the fact that she did not know why he had done what he had done, whatever it was, and that he had resolved, whether through fear or pride or depression, not to tell her. She loved her husband and shared his suffering through her labor. She gave all she could to help him, and she knew that he also strained within the confines of his affliction. Yet she could not reach him. Her love could not communicate itself to him regardless of how concentrated the effort. She gave all that she had and it was not enough.

I had come to Chile to work with the Fondación Cristo Vive, to learn what I could about life in the Recoleta slum and of the community effort there to resurrect itself. But I realized before many days had passed that the real purpose of my stay in Chile centered on my time with Carmen and Santiago. I do not mean to say that my work with the foundation was irrelevant—it was not. I consider many there as friends and count others as companions and teachers. But my days concentrated in a small apartment with a childless couple worried about meeting the next month's rent. Though I was able to offer help and friendship in la Recoleta, Santiago, and Carmen and I shared ourselves with each other, as much as that is possible. It was as if we had found one another, and we rested awhile together.

In spite of the despair surrounding the house, I found in the situation there a far more potent hope. My year devoted to hunting saints had brought me into their home and to a domestic heroism comparable to any other virtuous act I had witnessed. With an almost tragic devotion Carmen manifested everyday that final virtue of selfless love, a mindless generosity of all that one has. I had gone out seeking examples of goodness with the intention of holding them up as a standard and a light. I would speak about them. I would write about them. I, along with others, would learn of what heights our souls were capable of achieving from the account I would give. But without the illumination of a contemplative tradition or an enlightened social awareness, Carmen was doing all the things that a saint does without even thinking about it. She tended the sick and beaten, often having to deal with Santiago's impudence as an obstacle to caring for him as his body demanded. She worked for the poor and the poor were her own family, striving to hold onto the same apartment to avoid the upset of a move. She demanded an account of the reasonless suffering of the innocent, crying in worry and loneliness when no one else was around. The force of things had pushed her into working towards one end, the caring survival of her small family. Unsupported financially by siblings and in-laws, constantly subverted by Santiago's domineering mother who wanted her son to live with her again, Carmen continued to reach for his hand, to hold it in hers. She showed, without mind towards display, the necessity of goodness. When I look to her, I think of how ridiculous it is to wonder whether or not saintliness is possible. It has nothing to do with what may or may not be possible. The question concerns doing what is needed.

When I first came to Carmen and Santiago's coun-try the proficiency with which I spoke Spanish hardly matched that of a Chilean three-year-old. A professor of mine, Dr. Caroline Cunningham, had received an invitation to accompany me for two weeks, and her fluency facilitated my beginning time there. She became a valued consolation to Carmen. Her atten-tiveness made her an understanding listener, and her joyfully sociable spirit delighted in finding the twist or pun in even the most serious moments to lighten everyone's spirit. Happy to travel, happy to be of help, she made others happy.

On the day of our arrival Santiago was at his mother's house in the middle of a visit that would last several days. Because of her busyness trying to earn the money to cover living and medical costs, Carmen could not always give Santiago the time he needed every day. He would spend weeks at his mother's home, but her help often proved a point of stress as she used her hospitality as evidence of a greater love than Carmen could offer. Dealing with a jealous power struggle of which she wanted no part on top of everything else with which she had to deal drained her continually.

Our arrival relieved Carmen of some of her loneliness. She spent the majority of our meals recounting Santiago's troubles. He had been an athlete, the steeplechase champion of Chile in younger days and a competitor in the Pan-American Games hosted in Rio de Janeiro. Even until his stroke he ran everyday, up a small mountain, San Cristóbal, inside the city. But his job caused him excessive stress. His manager argued over commission every month. Santiago held his frustration until it broke him, ending in an almost total loss of speech, mild epilepsy, paralysis of his right side, and destroyed self-esteem. Carmen looked across the table from us the first night.

"To have been such a man," she said, flexing her muscles, imploring us to understand. "And then—" and her arms fell flaccid at her side, thinking she had failed to communicate his loss.

A few days later Dr. Cunningham and I returned from la Recoleta late in the afternoon. As we came in the door, Carmen surged from the dark hallway, running from her bedroom as she heard us enter.

"Oh, oh," she exclaimed, kissing us welcome on the cheek and tugging our hands to follow her. "He's here, Santiago is here and you can meet him."

She bottled her exuberance as best she could when she entered the bedroom. Like a parent trying to surprise her child with a new toy, she stalked slowly around the bed and leaned over the mound of rumpled sheets.

"Darling, Santiago," she smiled broadly, trying to make him envious of her secret. "There are some people here to see you." A confused noise came from the bed and then a gaunt face, freshly shaven, poked above the edge of the top blanket.

"Visitors, love. Our guests," Carmen whispered to encourage him, and a look of recognition sprung to his face. He had never seen us, never met us, but he had heard of us and knew we were coming. Suddenly embarrassed by his appearance he began hoisting himself up onto the pillow, struggling to make his bum hand move faster, fretting over whether to use his good hand to comb his hair or pull himself upright. He pressed himself into a sitting position and locked his weak right arm as a prop; the elbow buckled and he lurched down into the bed's backboard. Carmen scrambled with the pillows to support him and then patted his hair down. "There, there," she whispered, and once he felt himself in position, Santiago glanced once to her for confidence and looked at us again. We still stood in the doorway, palms sweating from wanting to help and being hindered by embarrassment to actually do anything.

He smiled at us, an awkward grin bent lopsided

by his paralysis. He seemed boyish. Above thin cheeks, his large eyes looked for approval. We smiled back eagerly, and he looked away.

There is a joy in speaking a language other than one's own. Maneuvering the constructions of the world, all of the meaning built upon words and expressions, becomes a game. In basketball, once the rules and technique on which skills are built are understood, play becomes flow, improvisation on a basic theme. Language functions similarly. Once the tongue unties words and grammatical construction, the rest is jazz.

Energized by that playfulness one can talk for hours about nothing and still feel stimulated to go on speaking. Like everyone else in the room, Dr. Cunningham could feel the strain of the moment weighing on us. Santiago wanted to speak and barely could. Already embarrassed by his appearance, paralysis disabled him completely. Carmen wanted us to cheer him, to rekindle his old hopes by our exoticism and happiness. We wanted to help without patronizing anyone. The room warmed uncomfortably with so much expectation and with growing disappointment. But Dr. Cunningham knew how to play. Her joy would become our joy if it could only be evoked. She picked up the ball and chucked it to Santiago.

"Hey, you must be the famous Santiago," she called across the room.

"M-m-e? Yes," he gestured limply to his chest. "Sa-n-ti-a-go..."

"Well we have heard so much about you," she showered enthusiasm on him as she moved to his side. Carmen started situating chairs for us all to sit

closer together. "I'm la Carolina, and this is Scott."
I smiled timidly and stepped closer.

"He-ll-o," he replied.

"Hello, hello," she said, her laughter like hands
massaging the tension out of the room.

"He-l-l-o," he repeated.

"I'll say hello again," she joked. "But only once
more. So, hello, and that's it. How has your day
been?"

"Good," Santiago stammered. "It's been good."

"Good, and ours was too," she continued, and for
the next hour and a half she sat by his bedside, chatting about the city, teasing him about sharing its
name, talking about the children at the nursery where
we worked, lamenting the failings of the United States
despite Santiago's generous protestations. Carmen
watched entranced, as if a very bad movie had suddenly taken a turn for the better.

As she went on talking, Santiago would occasionally turn to me and ask, "And you?"

"His Spanish is better than he thinks," Dr.
Cunningham would vouch for me, flattering as she
explained. "But he speaks French much better. So
he's learning, and soon he'll be ready to say more."
More would be something as opposed to silence.

"No, a li-ttle," Santiago insisted, turning again
to me.

"No, no," I would respond, explaining everything
in the one Spanish word I was sure to pronounce
well.

As their conversation continued, Dr. Cunningham
noticed Santiago rubbing his right arm. He would
start at the fingers and clench them in his left fist,

move across his palm and down his forearm, up to his shoulders and back down again.

"What are you doing?" she asked him.

"This, this," he said, slapping his arm. "No good, no, no..."

Carmen stepped in to explain, relieving him of his mounting frustration with the words. "To make his arm stronger," she said tenderly.

"Your skin looks so smooth," Dr. Cunningham remarked. Santiago smiled shyly. The compliment must have confused itself with the intimations of femininity that unweathered skin evokes to cause him to blush so deeply. "Can I touch it?" she asked.

With his left hand he lifted his right arm and laid it across his belly. Then he lifted his hand with the left one and held it out for her.

"Feel it," she said to me, and I touched along the thin bones behind his palm. A little lotion still remained to be absorbed from the surface.

"Like this?" she asked, and he nodded as she massaged the thick palm muscle below the thumb.

She handed me his hand. "Like...this?" I asked, repeating the sounds I had understood her to have made. My effort excited Santiago.

"Yes, yes, li-ke...thi-s." He looked happily to Carmen.

"It makes him stronger, to do that," she said. "Excuse me," and she left the room to dry her eyes.

"It's okay?" I asked Santiago, continuing to work his hand.

"Yes." He watched my hands and then my face for a few moments.

I placed his arm across his belly and stood up.

Walking to the other side of the bed I climbed onto it, seating myself cross-legged by Santiago's side. I picked up his right arm again and lay it across my lap, placing both hands on his shoulder and beginning to massage. Even so high up his skin felt silken, so thin I feared I might tear it when I pulled long through the muscles.

Dr. Cunningham was leaning forward on her knees, watching us. She turned her head up to Santiago, whose eyes had remained riveted on me. I looked at her.

"It's all right?" she asked him.

"Yes," he said.

Everyday that Santiago was at the apartment I would sit with him, talking lightly or watching soccer on television. He needed to practice speaking and my language was so poor that I did not frustrate him with complicated conversation to which he could not respond, and he didn't intimidate me with the long spaces between his words. I hung on every expression, even repeating them sometimes to try to get them right. As we sat, I rubbed his arm, working the muscles to prevent atrophy.

At times his spirit would surge in all its independence. One afternoon as he was preparing to bathe, Santiago resolved to no longer rely upon Carmen when he washed. He insisted that she not scrub him, that she not shampoo his hair, that she not support him as he climbed in and out of the tub or as he toweled off. Wanting for him to progress in therapy, loving his independence, Carmen nonetheless feared letting go of him, literally. A fall might retard what advances he had made, especially if he hit his head. But he would give no ground, straining so hard to say just the word "No" clearly that his face flushed red and the tendons in his neck strung out like ropes. She relented, finally, and knocked on my door in the next room where I'd heard the argument.

"Scott?" she called and peeked around the door's edge.

"Carmen. Yes?"

"Scott," she whispered and entered. I sat up to listen. "Would you help me? Santiago wants to bathe alone, he doesn't want my help, and that's good. It is, it is very good. For him to do it alone. You understand? Good, well. Still, I'm very worried. And I wanted to ask you, would you please just stand outside the bathroom door and listen in case he needs anything?"

"Yes, yes, of course." I started to stand.

"Oh, not yet," she said, taking an anxious step towards me. "Wait until he's already in there. Then just listen. But don't let him know. Okay?"

I could hear Santiago fumbling in the clothes closet next door, sighing loudly to himself, trying to form thoughts into words. "Of course."

I situated a chair at the entrance of my bedroom and picked up my book again. Santiago called to Carmen to help him take off his clothes and put on a robe. Therein lay the hardest blow to his ego, it seemed to me. He would resolve to surpass a given obstacle, to assert himself towards returning as much as possible to his former state. But somewhere in the process a small detail would arise. A shoe would need to be tied, toothpaste squeezed, or a bottle opened. Suddenly the success of his entire pursuit would again rely on someone else's help.

As I heard him shuffling toward the door I stood up and turned to look down the hall. Head down, he concentrated on placing his right foot even with his left, then fully in front of his left. Then he gripped the wall and supported himself as he swung his left foot forward quickly and shifted his weight onto it before the right leg gave out.

When I moved he noticed me. I looked at him, smiled, and stepped back into my room. Heat rushed over me. I felt traitorous spying on him like that, secretly standing as the safety net he did not want —I, the guest and surrogate son. No apology was possible. I hadn't the language skill or the desire to betray Carmen. She didn't need me to discredit the allowance she had given him with this opportunity to clean himself. I waited listening till the door to the bathroom closed, and I looked down the hall. Light shone beneath the door and I heard his feet shuffling on the other side. The washing machine rocked unbalanced as he shifted his hand on it for support.

I left my book on the table and sat down on the hall floor, leaning my back against the wall. For a while Santiago mumbled half broken incoherencies to himself, looking for words lost in the gap between his clear thoughts and his lagging tongue. Then the water shot on and covered every sound except its splattering against his body.

I put my head back and closed my eyes. Thoughts streamed as they would have had I stood under the same shower. The image of Jarune, more like an icon than a photograph in my memory, came back to me. I remembered working with him, watching his eyes to know how to touch him, moving slowly over his body, over his dissipated muscles.

Maybe the water had brought him back to my mind, especially the vision I still hold of his wife rinsing his hair so tenderly. They had understood something that connected them and enabled them to touch in the way that they did, so tenderly, as if they had both accepted the same thing. Perhaps the certainty of their situation made it easier for them to agree on the simplicity of love. Santiago's fight and frustration could hold him in isolation, preventing him from touching Carmen, or her from touching him, with the same knowing. But the more I tried to analyze the parallels and divergences between the two men and the two couples, the more clearly I saw how little I understood of their lives.

The color of their hair and skin; their withered limbs; their impoverished words and my meager comprehension; the movement of my hands; their thankfulness and their age—at times returning from work in the afternoon to Santiago seemed like walking into a room and finding Jarune in it. Santiago, worried and ignorant of facts, feared that he had somehow contracted HIV. When he expressed those concerns I would sometimes feel even a bit bitter, as if his persistent nightmare insulted those I knew almost certainly to be dead, Jarune and Prichya foremost.

At no other time was I invited into such an intimate place with another person. In Thailand, Jarune lay before me everyday, naked and dying. Prichya exposed the infection in his groin area that he would not show anyone else. Together they called me into the singleminded search for integration into the perfection underlying life. For whatever reason, whether as a guest in his home or a trusted confidant, because I had touched him physically or because as a visitor his secret would disappear with my departure, Santiago also opened up to me.

One day as I sat with him massaging his arm he jerked up his head to look me in the eyes.

"It doesn't work anymore," he said gravely.

"What?" I asked with a grin. I hadn't caught all of the Spanish.

"It doesn't work anymore." He pulled his body up and at a diagonal, moving his torso away from me so as to see me better.

"It doesn't work...anymore? Okay. Wait." I looked at him a moment. "Wait. I don't understand. What doesn't work anymore?"

With his good hand he flung his right hand off of the covers and to the side. He pushed down the sheets as far as he could and then kicked his legs to move them further off. I sat up straighter and reached to help him pull them from his legs, but he cut me short.

"Look," he said curtly. His eyes grieved. His left hand yanked on the elastic waistband of his sweatpants, tugging them past his belly button and where they caught between the bed and his hips until the beginning of his pubic hair showed like a black, silvery nest.

"See?" he pressed. "It doesn't work anymore."

Although Carmen must surely have known all this and more, in that moment I felt certain that Santiago had never spoken those words to anyone else. He needed another person to know the extent of his devastation. If I could not feel his isolation, at least I could know of it, and of the urgency he felt pressing inside his chest.

It was then that I knew Santiago would recover, though to what degree I did not know and still do not.

He wanted to overcome that which bound him from others. He raged against it. All of his frustration over language, over saying just the word "Yes" clearly, was born from that deeply seeded need.

I reflect on the connection between Jarune and his wife. I remember his eyes and his fatigue. Everything spoke of endings, of resignation, and I wonder if their shared understanding was not a willingness to be with each other despite all history, complaint and memory, free of all the usual fetters. They were together, and that was enough.

For Santiago and Carmen that simple acceptance could not suffice. Their connection could not surpass the barriers imposed by illness, at least not wholly. They had to come through them, all because Santiago had resolved to live and to live better.

On a bus in the city, a friend from work at the foundation asked me how my time in Chile pleased me.

"It's going so well," I mused and looked off to the mountains behind their curtain of smog. "It's like I'm walking on the border of something so perfect, like I'm in exactly the right place."

"A nice place to be at the end of such a trip." She perked her eyebrows quizzically. "But, it's not too hard at home? In Chile, I mean, with your host father sick?"

I explained briefly about Jarune, about massaging Santiago's arm. "See?" I looked further out the window. "It's like a resurrection."

The Saints

A few yards past a realistic sculpture dedicated to the police of Santiago and built at the end of the Pinochet dictatorship, on the city's main avenue, Dr. Cunningham and I perused the craft booths of local artisans. Cheap copper trinkets and tourist medallions tinkled in the morning breeze. Everything has its beauty in a certain light.

She fell into talking with an older vendor. From the throat of his three sweaters he croaked about politics, money, food, and politics.

Suddenly, breaking the course of the conversation completely, he blurted out, "They killed my son in '88!"

His voice resumed its previous low tones, and they talked on a few minutes more.

How we provide the needed space for confessions and testimonies, I do not know. The voice comes pressing up from inside. Listen.

Port-au-Prince and the Fondwa Valley, Haiti

1 – 14 July 1999

Where every bone is broken,
Where hopelessness runs as blood,

I have witnessed, even there,
Our body standing
To brace the mountain in its place.

Haiti is an eroded country. When the economy went from a standard of subsistence to desperation decades ago, people began scraping the ground for any possible means of sustenance. One afternoon while walking along a mountain footpath, I saw a rope tied to a stout tree and hanging tautly, at a sharp angle. I walked to the road's edge and peered down into the valley. Beneath my nose a man poured sweat, hacking away at the mountainside with his hoe. Rotten rows of corn stumps fell under his blows as he turned the ground over for a new season. We saluted each other in country fashion.

"How is it?" he hollered up to me, raising his straw hat to fan himself and wave to me with one swoop.

"Not so bad, is it?" I shouted back with a smile.

"Oui!" he piped in the shrill falsetto every farmer, male and female, uses to end the normal chorus of greetings.

It rained later that afternoon, a powerful Caribbean storm that rounded up twenty wayfarers caught on the road and herded us together, drenched and laughing, under a low porch for over two hours. The gale stretched out its hands and ran its fingers against the grain of the farmer's rows, ripping his furrows down the side of the valley. After the storm I walked with an agronomist and a community activist to survey the damage. The storm had not been strong enough to cause harm to permanent structures, but the ground had been scoured bare. In the valley bottom a narrow creek ran amply, slothful as it dragged its new weight of silt and mud.

"The grade of the mountains can't retain loose soil, so just when it's time to plant and the storms come, another covering is lost," Edrise, who worked for the Peasant Farmer's Association of the Fondwa Valley (APF) as a community organizer and educator, explained to me. He pointed to an uprooted bean plant, locally known as pois congo. "We've started to mix cultures so that a variety of plants both use and replenish the soil, and they help to staple the earth down when one crop is being harvested. But we still lose a lot. And the families can't afford to let any land sit fallow because money and food are so scarce. And with so few trees, it's hard to manage the erosion at all."

It is said that Haiti could feed itself thirty years ago. But surplus goods from the United States then began to flood the market. Sold at the cheapest prices, the products undercut whatever Haitian competition already existed. Rice, the staple of the Haitian diet, also once formed the largest industry on the island. When Blue Ribbon rice began its shipments out of Miami, however, workers began to disappear from the fields. The business could not sustain its employees and eventually collapsed.

With no production and no work, fewer and fewer had the means with which to purchase goods, an economic paradox since an increasing number of goods were imported. The decline into ever worsening poverty continues to plague the country.

Many sought alternative means of income by making and selling charcoal. As the primary source of fuel in Haiti, charcoal sells easily. After cutting a given number of trees, the lumber is left to smolder under a mound of damp earth, burning down over the course of a few days until it is ready to be bagged and taken to market.

The result is a denuded country. Photographs of the border between Haiti and the Dominican Republic show a clear line dividing the two countries. To the east, lush tropical forests roll across mountains. The Haitian side is brown from deforestation. Called desertification, the gradual loss of verdure and of fertile soil leaves some areas resembling the Sahara. Though not unified into a massive region, splotches of bleached, sandy country nonetheless dot the landscape.

There is also a form of human erosion in Haiti. As occurs in many countries with one major urban center, the capital of Port-au-Prince draws its people out of the hills and into its streets. The dream of city life dies hard in the mouths of peasants, and many still come expecting to find a better life through employment. They imagine that if the land cannot sustain everyone, perhaps the city can.

Hundreds of international relief organizations, religious and humanitarian, have heard the call of Haiti and seek to provide some assistance there. But the majority of them become mired in Port-au-Prince and never extend their operations into the countryside. Thus a second drain forms, pulling more Haitians into the city, with the offer of free food and medical care that helps them briefly but sustains no one. A U.S. botanist working in the countryside for over twenty years has described Port-au-Prince as the country's black hole.

The result sprawls into the bay. Slums degrade into even worse shanty towns, while the bourgeoisie press higher up the mountains circling the city. All the filth accumulated in the streets streams down the hills of Port-au-Prince into the flats of the poorest neighborhoods when it rains. There it sits among the people dragged by their country's storms out of the mountains and into squalor.

I have never known a country more beautiful. The grace with which people walk down the city's streets is only matched by the burning blue of the mountains' beauty. In the Fondwa Valley where I worked, the steep hills form a rim that opens toward the southern city of Jacmel, invisible from the road, like a mouth. Only South African sunlight passes over the landscape with comparable intensity, a clarity like clean thought, as if it were water poured gradually from an enormous bowl, washing across the green and dying rock. Haiti is a beautiful, beautiful country.

I was aware of at least the basic outline of these ideas before arriving in Port-au-Prince. Through discussions with professors and a vague consciousness of the turmoil surrounding Jean-Bertrand Artistide's election to the presidency and the ensuing coup d'état in 1991, I had learned the broadest contours of Haiti's suffering. In the years before being awarded the Presidential Scholarship, when I would consider the possibility of receiving the honor and dream of where I might go, Haiti always came to mind before all other countries. Centuries of economic neglect, political abuse, and racist victimization had made its people the epitome of need in my mind. If the scholarship intended to school me in saving humanity via a tour through the worst the world had to offer, there was no better place to go.

But arranging a visit to Haiti proved difficult despite the ample resources provided by the scholarship. The problem lay in the simple obstacle of finding a contact—faxes would not go through, e-mails and letters seemed to disappear somewhere between South Carolina and the Caribbean. Long after I had confirmed all of my other international connections, establishing even the first line of communication with anyone in Haiti continued to elude me.

It was not, in fact, until the second week of my stay in Chile that a visit seemed realistically possible. Because of Haiti's reputation for violence and unpredictability, I had promised the trip's sponsors that I would not go there unless I had reached a person or an organization who in turn invited me to come. Tickets were purchased in the event that something turned up. But as I went through the course of months toward the end of June, when I would leave Chile, I became increasingly convinced that Haiti was denied me. No lead came through.

But the good word fell from the sky one afternoon down in a basement internet café in downtown Santiago. Somehow, through divine dabbling in the cyber grapevine, notice of my desire to know Haiti had been passed along until a volunteer at the Washington, DC, Church of the Savior's Ministry of Money responded to my plea for help. He sent me the e-mail address of Anne Hastings, the supervising director of Fonkoze Microcredit Bank for the Organized Poor, based in Port-au-Prince.

I wrote her as soon as I had read the message from Washington, and her response seemed just as immediate. She invited me enthusiastically, confessing that she had no idea how I could help but assuring me that something would be found for me to do.

I walked out of the café into the late afternoon chill of Chilean winter, exhilarated. Even the city's exhaust filled my lungs sweetly, I felt so satisfied. My mind spun trough thoughts until it reached the pseudo-artistic imaginings in which it dearly loves to indulge. Haiti would complete my journey, I pondered, not only chronologically but thematically, poetically. With AIDS like Chiang Mai, poverty like Bihar, violence like Palestine, African heritage like Durban, and a history of bungling U.S. intervention like Chile, Haiti would consummate my trip, encapsulating every struggle, every broken soul, every virtuous act of the past seven months in the body of one little half-island country. Like a maraschino cherry precisely placed, Haiti awaited my arrival with poised perfection.

Because I did not know I could go to Haiti until so late in the trip, and because when I did know I conceived of it almost as a summarizing flourish, an epilogue sealing with conciseness what I had already established, my month in Chile seemed to me like the final leg. My stay in Haiti would last only two weeks anyway.

Throughout June heavy smog had covered Santiago. Surrounded by the Andes, Chile's capital experiences a temperature inversion in the winter that traps the city's exhaust over itself. Brownish-gray soot smudges the yellow municipal buses roaring recklessly down La Alameda, the main avenue. The noses of the children with whom I worked in la Recoleta ran black. Some days, when a breeze would pick up, or early in the morning before traffic got too heavy, the mountains could be glimpsed, massive and lined up like soldiers waiting to descend on the streets. They stood in two rows, the lower cordillera encircling the city and behind them, the Andes proper, full in stature.

The smog would clear with rain, I was often told, but rain eluded us. The region had suffered drought for three years and so, despite their elevation and the winter season, only the highest, most distant peaks showed traces of snow when they were visible at all. The mountains were as brown as the tires of the city's taxis.

But I awoke to the sound of rain against my window on the morning of the last full day in Santiago. Clouds hid the tops of high-rises, scraping themselves open wide and emptying themselves on the pavement. It poured all day. That evening I fell asleep to the sound of sloshing through gutters and then woke, sometime in the night, to stillness.

When I woke again later, though still early in the morning, I rubbed a blanket against the window to clear the night's condensation and looked across the skyline. Clouds still crowded the sky with a sleek, bluish cotton filling that hardened into a rock of gray at the bottom.

"Look, Scott," Carmen whispered through my cracked door. "Snow. They have snow."

I looked again and laughed. Almost indistinguishable from the white sky, the mountains paraded new snow, row after row, in greater number than I had ever seen. The lowest and closest ones looked like ice cream bars with all but the bottom of the chocolate fudge bitten off and only the vanilla cream showing. I took a bus to Los Dominicos, a quarter on the city's perimeter much closer to the mountains, to see them better.

I could not have been happier. I have always understood the mountains as perfection, a standing ideal of clarity and unassuming grandeur towards which we aspire. And here, on the last day of my trip, with only the Haitian chorus to be sung, the Andes had washed themselves, dressed in their finest, and stood up to bid me farewell. I had said good-bye to my host father Santiago and intuited that the road before him was good. In him Jarune lived again for me; in him the hope of my trip had not died. And the mountains rose up to confirm the perfection of it all.

On the bus I pressed against the window, peering out to see the peaks between breaks in the buildings. I pulled the collar of my jacket over my mouth to heat myself with my breath. Even in the bus I was chilled. I stuck my hands into the sleeves of their opposite arm, like a monk.

As I rubbed my hands together to warm them up, a finger ran over a fingernail. I stopped and felt the nail again, letting the soft finger padding brush slowly over its curve. I looked down and pulled my hands out to inspect them.

Like lines cut in rock by straight running water and just as smooth, a clear little ridge ran down the middle of my right thumb. I saw the same ridge on the other thumb, then carefully rotated my hand to see the flat light in the bus shine on a row of indentations faceting my thumbnail all the way to the cuticle. I shivered. I was sweating in my jacket, my armpits itching from the heat, and the moisture had chilled me. Heat like fear crawled up past my collar along my jaw line, behind my ears, across my scalp. I was afraid.

In Thailand, Phra Au had lent me a book on physical ailments common to people suffering from HIV and AIDS, including graphic illustrations of visible abnormalities symptomatic of AIDS related complications. On that bus in Chile, my mind jumped back through the pages filled with photographs of fingernails deformed by fungi, toenails leprous and disintegrating.

One picture had shown fingernails so ridged that it looked as if someone had carved furrows into the nail with a linoleum knife. My nails were ridged, not dramatically but clearly nonetheless, and I had never before noticed that about them. I lay my head against the window and closed my eyes with a deliberateness meant to convince my speeding, one-track thoughts that fear need no longer fuel them, that the situation was in hand. But I was afraid.

I had gone on this trip to help and to learn. To be honest, I had hoped to join those saints I sought through it, serving the needy, spreading the good news of their freedom by virtue of loving acts. But in my fear I saw the trip as having become too much a part of me. It was inside me, sure as death. It had filled my veins for seven months without my ever realizing it. If I was sick, and I was so scared I could hardly stave off the thought, the journey had filled my body—all these people and places and flights and needs. I would not be able to leave it. I would not be able to stop it.

I thought of Haiti with distrust, almost as if the country in my mind had betrayed me. It was supposed to finish things, tie up loose ends, complete the theme through its complete misery. And here I sat, on a bus headed for pure snow, afraid that I had become more of a Haiti than the country itself. No matter how much I reasoned, I could not convince myself that I was thinking foolishly, that I was wrong. I worked myself into exhaustion.

Three weeks later, back at home, the doctor chuckled at my concern while the nurse pricked my finger. He reassured me that I had nothing to fear, and later the tests proved him right. But sitting in the laboratory, my finger pressing blood into stout little vials,

I remembered how intense the cold felt when I stepped off the bus. I was as close to the mountains as the route would take me, and I could only stand to look up at them for a moment before beginning to walk to the next bus stop to stay warm. They could not have seemed more purely white and stable, clean, or more distant.

Haiti: the Church

"There's no place like Haiti, that's for sure," Sister Anne shook her head in amusement. She passed the box of crackers to Sister Ellen, who chuckled knowingly. "The sense of humor these people have, it's incredible. A black sense of humor, really dark."

The racist pun in her comment was not intended maliciously. That she used a joke's discriminatory language to praise the people with whom she worked illustrated her point. She wanted to testify to the ability of Haitians to resist, often successfully, even the most difficult situations.

I sat on a second floor balcony looking over the lowest hills of Port-au-Prince into the bay. Fresh off the plane from Miami, the minivan from the Hospice St. Joseph had scooped me up just before the crowd of taxi and tap-tap drivers swallowed me. A hospitality house run by two U.S. American nuns dedicated to building U.S.—Haitian relations by hosting visiting church groups and volunteers during their stay in the city, the hospice also serves as a base of operations for an extensive school program and a free medical clinic run on the grounds. I arrived around noon and had hardly gotten the chance to shake the dust off my pants before Sister Anne swung by my room.

"We're just about to have our lunch," she said, speaking through the open blinds into my room. "It's not much, but we'd be glad to have you join us."

I'd stopped turning down food and conversation in English months ago, and their eagerness to swap stories for my benefit spiced the meal where the peppered cheese came up short. They had both committed themselves to life in Haiti as a sign and a practice of solidarity with its people, and they had both lived through the coup that deposed Aristide and the military dictatorship that followed him.

"During that time," Sister Ellen explained, "any activity that supported potential opponents of the military or the bourgeoisie were certain to be targets of violence. And here we were running our medical clinic. They never actually shot up the building here, but everyday at fairly regular times, someone would shoot off a round right outside the gates. And aside from the clinic, we were hiding refugees who'd had to go underground. So you can imagine, all those people in hiding tucked back in our hallways, and then a burst of gunfire goes off right by their heads, on the other side of the wall, you can see that it got pretty tense around here sometimes."

But the sisters weren't just telling me war tales to give me a little scare before I ventured out into the streets. They wanted to help me form an idea of the people, at least of the poor, the majority of the population. Sister Anne took up the story.

"One day I was back there with some of the ones in hiding. You have to understand that many of these people had never seen a flush toilet or running water before, so they would leave things running all night long without knowing they had to turn them off. And that meant a lot of mopping, and constantly reminding people the faucet had to be turned back.

"Well I was back in the hall, mopping, probably, and I heard the strangest sound out in the courtyard. I couldn't tell what it was, and so I went out onto the balcony here to look down. And down there on the driveway everyone was in a circle, all looking down. The clinic was running then and these were all people that had come to be checked on, or their family members that had come to be with them. And everyone was gathered into this circle, so there must have been at least fifty people down there. Don't you think, Ellen?"

"Oh fifty, at least. Probably lots more than that," she confirmed.

"So I was looking down, trying to figure out what was going on," Sister Anne continued. "And I realized that the sound I heard was laughter. Everybody was down there laughing, all the people in line because they're sick or hurt, maybe wounded by a vigilante or soldier. All laughing.

"And one man was in the center of the circle, lying down on the pavement. I could hear him above everyone else, laughing and sputtering what he had to say in between fits of laughter. You won't believe what he was doing, flopping around on the ground out there.

"He had been beaten that morning by a group of soldiers, and he was acting out what they had done to him. He pointed to his elbow—'They got me here,' he said. 'And here, and here, and then they stuck their

clubs here,' going through all they had done to him."
Sister Anne gestured to her legs, her hips, to suggest
the man's awkward dance.

"And all the while he's laughing and laughing, and
everyone else is laughing too. Mind now, all this
happened that same morning, and they had really put
this guy through it.

"But he's laughing, and every once in a while he
shouts out, 'They did this, and they didn't kill me!
They hit me here, and I'm alive!' And everyone
laughed with him, like a big congregation around a
lunatic preacher."

"There's no place like Haiti, the way these people
make it through together. I don't think any of us
would make it a day without our sense of humor.
Whatever happens, it's not as bad as it could be."

Haiti: the Saints

"Why don't you go out to Fondwa with Corey for
a few days?" Anne Hastings suggested on my third
morning of work at Fonkoze. After flipping through
photo albums and devouring what literature existed
on the bank's establishment and mission, it quickly
became apparent that my hands could accomplish
little at the office in Port-au-Prince.

Anne's son, Corey, had come to Haiti to assist
with the foundation of a bakery in the Fondwa Valley,
south of the capital, by serving as its manager. A
group of men from the farming community had
wanted to start the business rather than continue
their region's reliance on bread trucked into the
mountains from Port-au-Prince, thereby increasing

bread quality and freshness as well as keeping their money in their own hills. Corey would manage the business only long enough to ensure its firm establishment and to train one of the farmers to take his position.

During a pause in her harried schedule, Anne had explained to me that the connection between the bakery and Fonkoze was more than simply economic.

"On a financial level, the bank loans capital to the bakery in order to encourage its growth," she said and briefly outlined the mechanics of how the loans were made and paid. "With the bakery everything has worked very well. But the bakery is part of a community development project through the Peasant Association of Fondwa, and that organization and this bank were both started by Father Joseph Philippe. So he began both and still serves as their director, and one feeding the other makes it possible."

On our way out to Fondwa, Corey raised his voice above the wind and the rattle of the pickup to tell me more about Father Joseph. He had grown up in Fondwa and left only to pursue his seminary education, a path that led him to Quebec, France, and the United States. During the Haitian democratic movement of the late '80s and '90s, he witnessed the assassinations and disappearances of countless fellow clergy and was himself forced into exile. But after Aristide's return to power, Father Joseph came back determined to contribute to the empowerment of the populace and the construction of a better Haiti.

The microcredit bank, Fonkoze, is the only bank accessible to the Haitian poor. It is also the only bank in Haiti with branches throughout the country. Most are located in only Cape Haitian and Port-au-Prince, the two largest metropolitan areas.

The Asosyasyon Peyizan Fondwa (APF) seeks to cultivate democratic involvement of the valley's inhabitants in solving communal problems. The activities connected to the association include the bakery, a newly constructed pigsty meant to be shared as a source of fertilizer, a medical clinic, literacy programs, and an orphanage.

"He wanted to come back home," Corey stated admiringly. The truck rose out of the Plain of Leogane into the blue, semi-denuded mountains. "He had to make sure that Fondwa was cared for."

When we arrived in Fondwa, the truck pulled up a gravel driveway and parked under spreading shade trees. A white building stood overlooking the valley beneath us, and from another building, dark and unpainted, the aroma of fresh bread poured. Corey jumped from the truck and stepped into the bakery, reappearing moments later and wiping flour off his hands.

"Let's have lunch," he smiled, and I followed him into the white building's entrance. A roadside restaurant, this also had only recently opened as another project born as a co-effort of Fonkoze and APF.

Over a plate of beans and plantains with thin chicken legs on the side, we stopped talking and sat in the cool quiet. A breeze cut the latticed corner of the porch and toyed with the tablecloth edges. Fondwa spread at our feet, ridge falling back upon ridge like the waves in the ocean beyond them. The closest mountains looked the golden color of water under the noon light. Those behind began green and turned into blue the bright color of the seared sky. Another pickup truck rumbled into the quiet. Still at the table, Corey looked out through the porch screening and nodded in the truck's direction.

"I didn't think you'd meet him this soon," he said.

As the three passengers left the vehicle and came towards the restaurant, the early afternoon quiet broke completely. People began appearing from the bakery, from the street, from under the shade trees, and from the corner of the building where I hadn't seen anyone previously. Everyone was talking, shaking hands. They all wanted a word with the man walking in front. The three men entered and sat. Soon the cook placed three plates with the same meal we had just eaten and a plastic pitcher of water before them. A crowd surrounded them. People came and went, but there were always people, and all of them talking. A basket of sliced white bread from the bakery was pushed to the center of the table, and three men began eating eagerly.

Corey had gone over to sit with them and then excused himself to go to the bakery, but I remained in my seat. I did not know them, I had not been asked to their table, and I had nothing to say. Instead, I watched them, trying to catch what Creole I could and chewing slowly to give myself an excuse to sit there longer.

In the middle of a bite, the man to whom everyone had wanted to speak sat straight up, paused, then turned causally around and said in clear English, "You must be Scott. Come, let me speak with you. I'm glad you're here."

I moved a chair next to his and sat. He placed his

hand flat on the red-checkered tablecloth.

"Here we are," he said matter-of-factly, patting his hand on the table. He looked at it as he spoke, then paused to gaze into the air momentarily. Grey ringed his eyes, as if his rich brown skin aged only there.

"And the problem," he continued, moving his other hand just below the table's lip, "is that the water is down here. So how can we bring the water up here, and also out to houses through here?" He swirled his hand around, indicating the valley. "How long are you here?" he asked, looking up from his charaded model to catch my eye momentarily.

"Two weeks in Haiti, but only a few days in Fondwa," I answered, still trying to get a sense of what he was talking about.

"That's good—just stay out here for a few days, maybe a week or so. Talk to people. Get their opinions. Take pictures, then you can go back to the United States and find someone able to help us build the water pump." He looked back at his hand thoughtfully. "I thought about a motor to pump the water, but who would maintain it?" For another moment he remained pensive. Then he turned to me abruptly, smiled, and said, "That's good. So we'll get water up here. And now we've got to go." He motioned to his companions and rose to walk out of the restaurant, waving thanks to the cook and chewing a last bite of plantain.

So it was that I was anointed and charged with documenting water needs in the Fondwa Valley. Excited by the opportunity to stay longer in the mountains and to be of actual help even after returning home, I undertook the project energetically, shooting roll after roll of film of nothing but uncaptured sources and streams.

But I was also worried. I knew nothing about construction costs or methods, and determining community willingness to maintain whatever might be built was difficult. Opinions conflicted and my French could decipher only so much Creole. Above all, I didn't know where to begin seeking help once back in the United States.

"Oh, don't worry," Anne reassured me when I voiced my concerns to her several days later. "Father Joseph knows what he's doing. He figures the best way to get something done is to get a lot of people to do it, and eventually somebody will. So don't imagine the thirst of the whole valley is riding on you."

Haiti: the Body

Father Joseph carried word back to Port-au-Prince that my stay in Fondwa would extend longer than previously planned, and I was introduced to Edrise, an employee of APF who would serve to help me in whatever way needed, especially as a guide and a translator. We walked the spine of one of the valley's ridges along a packed dirt road to a boxy white concrete building. So prominent and unique to the valley that it can easily be spotted from almost any point in the region, the APF Cultural Center housed the organization's medical clinic and educational facilities, as well as a handful of guest quarters. Edrise showed me to my room.

"I've spoken with Siné," he told me from the

doorway. "He's a farmer with land nearby. He'll show you the source and piping that feed this area and the center tomorrow morning. So you can wait on the porch till he comes."

At around 9:30 the following day, a skinny old man strode slowly up the embankment to the open porch where I sat studying the landscape. Like a boy fascinated with the city outside his apartment but too timid to go down into the street, I gazed at the moving shadows blocked out by the clouds across the face of the blue hills. The man approached me without my noticing. He greeted me in Creole, grinning under his broken straw hat, and I scrambled to decipher what he had said and how I could respond. Modified French spilled out of my mouth haltingly, and he looked at me sideways.

"You speak Spanish?" he asked in the language.

"Very little," I responded.

"Good enough," he nodded and motioned for me to follow him.

We made our way along cow paths toward the springs. With the Spanish he had learned in Dominican sugar cane fields and that I had picked up from a girlfriend and a roommate, he pointed out the different crops cultivated on every plot—beans, corn, and mango trees, heavy with ripe fruit, everywhere. At the source he showed me how water is captured in a concrete encasement, then piped to a reservoir, a simple concrete box a few yards downhill. He motioned that everything had to be cleaned occasionally as we peered into the darkness through a hole in the metal lid.

"But the problem," he tried to make me understand, "is with keeping it all working. Because who will clean this? One person always? It must be everyone, sometimes, but who will work?" Above all, people neglected the care demanded by the piping system. Siné pointed out breaks in the tubing as we walked, gesturing that a mishandled hoe had chopped into the pvc, or that a cow's hoof had punctured it. The knob on a water distribution station's faucet had snapped off, and no water ran.

"Children," he said. "Turned too much, too far, and now nothing."

Over the next two weeks, I roamed the Fondwa Valley, learning and rewalking the turns in every path leading to water. A handful of sources had been captured already, but most suffered some damage that either limited their output or cut off the water supply entirely. Communities found themselves reliant on easily contaminated streams and pools, not nearly so safe as a piped spring. As best I could understand, every case supported Siné's frustrated accusation that the people were to blame due to their own carelessness. After a week of trips to water sources and interviews, I confided to Edrise my fears about the work Father Joseph had given me.

"The thing is, I'm not sure anyone from the U.S. will come to work here if people can't maintain what's built." I could see he understood, so I ventured further. "The idea of not only capturing a source but of routing the water uphill by using a motor isn't going to sound practical if nobody will fix the motor, or if nobody can."

"That not all," he said with a grim laugh. "In two of these communities there are a few people who do not like Father Joseph, so they sabotage all of the projects there. What is for their own good, they destroy." He stared at the concrete kitchen floor.

"I mean, I am trying to learn and I'll try when I return home. But I'm worried it might not work," I warned gently.

"Yes. But then, let me show you something. Come with me to Citronnier tomorrow. There is a community meeting you should see." I assured him I'd happily go.

The next afternoon we walked to the outskirts of the valley, an hour and a half from the APF center. Along the way he pointed to three hills on the opposite side of a thin stream, all golden with sand, completely barren of any vegetation.

"We call this 'The Desert,'" he said. "You see what cutting trees for charcoal does to us."

We continued on and came eventually to a small blue wooden house atop a hill. Unshucked corn hung from the branches of surrounding trees, drying. Beside the house an open-sided, thatched shelter held a few wooden chairs and two log benches. Already a group of nearly ten people, from adolescents to the elderly, had gathered. Edrise greeted them all warmly and introduced me. After a few stragglers arrived, everyone stood for a brief prayer, and the meeting began.

After a few moments, I lost track of the subject and fell back into a more detached, observant mode. I watched them talking to each other, farmers, husbands and wives, a school teacher, her students, all intent on what was going on. Animated but respectful, every person, from youngest to oldest, men and women had their say. I felt as if I were back in one of Nanty's township meetings in South Africa, as if the light passing through the breaks in the palm thatching illuminated us more deeply than our sunlit skin.

Edrise turned to me, and I noticed the meeting had paused. "They want you to know that they are willing to maintain a water source. I told them more about your research. They don't have a captured source because they live so far away from APF, but they say they will do the work." Someone spoke out briefly, and Edrise turned back to me. "They want to take you somewhere." He smiled encouragingly.

"Let's go," I said enthusiastically, and as I moved to stand the whole group rose as one person.

Epilogue: Haiti

We slipped down a muddy clay slope, winding steeply from the ridge on which the house sat to a stream below. We followed the water back to a low hill that showed similar deforestation. Only a stand of trees along its crest and spots of low brush covered with green its grainy surface.

"Here. This is the place," a man called out from behind me in the line.

A quiet tongue of water spilled over rocks in a small, grotto-like space at the hill's base.

"See," a woman beamed at me. "See what we have done?"

The spring ran down into a pool, hollowed out of the stream bed and widening. Rocks, mortared together with mud, retained water to calf depth.

"This is their source," Edrise said to me in a low

voice. "But see how dirty it might be after rain? With the runoff, and the cows walking everywhere." As he talked, children splashed two women in the stream below the pool. Another woman scooped a plastic white bucket full of water and hoisted it, resting it on a cloth coil on top of her head. She turned without speaking and made her way slowly back up the path we had just descended. Stirred sediment swirled in the pool, gradually settling.

"See what we have done. See?" another man called, pointing to the two packed dirt canals dug into the slope of the hill to channel run off. "We have done this!"

"They have done this," Edrise murmured, and he leaned over to rinse his face in the water his hands cupped.

Deserving Support...

During an address to Westerners concerned about the situation in Bihar, Sister Jessi once remarked, "If all you are going to give is money, you may as well throw it in the Bay of Bengal." Sincerely engaging a problem means committing ourselves, financially and otherwise, according to the responsibilities and means that we feel we have.

My familiarity with the work of individuals and organizations dedicated to social action and care has proven to be one of the greatest benefits of my year abroad. Having joined in helping them, I can vouch for their integrity and need. I hope that recording this account will serve to connect those with resources of time, money, skill, and vision with my hosts. A list of addresses for contacting those projects deserving and in need of support follows.

Friends for Life Foundation *(Baan Puen Cheewit)*
183 Moo 4
Suthep, Muang District
Chiang Mai, 50200
Thailand
tel/fax: +66-53-283272

Sister Jessi (**Mahisi Gyanodaya Abhiyan/ The Campaign for Awakening Wisdom**)
Burmese Vihar
Bodh Gaya, Bihar
824231, India
fax: 91-631-400-848 • tel: 91-631-400-881
> *The Bodhgaya Development Association (BDA) is an international organization that creates support for social upliftment projects in Bodh Gaya, including Sister Jessi's schools. Their website, **www.bit.net.au/~vheyde/bda/#MG**, lists contact information and explains the work that they assist.*

Bodhgaya Development Association (BDA)
147 Richmond Rd.
Morningside QLD 4170
Australia
tel: (+61-7)3399-2017
vheyde@bit.net.au

Re'ut Sadaka
Derech Allenby 20
33265 Haifa
Israel
fax: 00972-4-8528392 • tel: 00972-4-8526926
Reut@inter.net.il
> *Re'ut Sadaka hosts a very informative website at*
www.israelpages.co.il/reut

Atfaluna Society for Deaf Children
(Ms. Geraldine Shawa)
PO Box 44
72 Philistine St.
Gaza City
fax: 07-2828495 • tel: 07-2828495 & 07-2865468
atfaluna@trendline.co.il